BONSAI
THEORY
OF CHURCH
GROWTH

BONSAI THEORY OF CHURCH GROWTH

Ken Hemphill

Auxano
PRESS

Tigerville, South Carolina
www.AuxanoPress.com

I dedicate this book
to Carl and Ruby Hemphill
my mom and dad who spent fifty-five
fruitful years in local church ministry.
They taught me to love the Lord
and His Bride, the church.
They are now enjoying unimpeded access to the King.

CONTENTS

ACKNOWLEDGEMENTS

The original edition of The Bonsai Theory of Church Growth was published in 1991 by Broadman Press. It has undergone several revisions and printings since that date. For a few years the Georgia Baptist Convention made them available to pastors.

Its popularity has amazed me and for that reason we have decided to release this completely revised and updated version. Kenneth Priest, who has joined me in this endeavor, was a moving force, in getting me to consider a new version of this book. He has found the material to be especially effective in getting churches to see their current situation and to devise strategies to overcome the artificial barriers which keep the church from reaching its full potential.

I want to thank my wife and partner in ministry, Paula who has been my helpmate for over 40 years. She is my inspiration and contributes immeasurable to all of my writing projects in more ways than one can imagine.

My children and my grandchildren are the joy of my life. We now have seven grandchildren and are awaiting number eight. Tina and Brett Bosch are the proud parents of Lois and Micah. Rachael and Trey Oswald enjoy their days with Emerson, Ward, and Ruby (named for my mom). Katie and Daniel Banks have two girls, Aubrey and Sloane, and are awaiting daughter number three.

It is an honor to publish with Auxano Press whose mission it is to provide biblically sound tools at an affordable price to help individuals and their churches to experience balanced growth. Kenneth Priest, project manager for Auxano Press has joined me in this revision by providing helpful tools to help the church implement the 6-week study and to make practical application to the local church setting.

We have used footnotes sparingly but Kenneth and I have learned from author's too numerous to mention.

You can find free small group study guides for The Bonsai Theory of Church Growth online free from Auxanopress.com. We pray that this book and the accompanying study guides will produce kingdom growth in your church.

Ken Hemphill
Travelers Rest, South Carolina
Spring 2011

INTRODUCTION: A PASSION FOR BONSAI

Several years ago I developed a passion for bonsai trees. Bonsai are nothing more than miniature versions of real trees. I'm not sure what spurred my interest. Perhaps it's somewhat genetic. My dad was always interested in all sorts of plants. Even though he lived in North Carolina he grew pineapples, oranges, coffee trees, and other assorted tropical and traditional plants. Truthfully, I never exhibited a real interest or knack for plants while under my dad's roof. Maybe this sort of genetic input takes time to mature. I guess it was a latent recessive gene.

Looking back, the movie *The Karate Kid* may have been the stimulus that kicked my "growing-plants-gene" out of neutral and into drive. My middle daughter, Rachael, was taking karate lessons at the time and we saw the film together. While she was impressed with the karate kicks and punches, I was fascinated by the miniature trees.

Not long after that movie I was on my *annual* family shopping trip to the mall. Malls are not my thing, and shopping is certainly not a favorite pastime for me. I dutifully trudged into and out of various clothing and toy stores according to the age of whichever daughter had me in tow. I was at the point of physical and financial exhaustion when I spotted a live bonsai. Actually, I discovered a table full of bonsai trees.

I was fascinated by the tiny trees before me. They *looked* like real trees! They *were* real trees! I began to inquire concerning their care and feeding, and ah yes, price. The girls soon became bored with my lack of enthusiasm for shopping. They were quickly dispatched to nearby stores to browse while I continued to inspect tree after tree. Finally, after much deliberation, I bought a small pine tree in a shallow blue pot. Little did I suspect that this decorative shallow pot was one of the keys to the mystery of the bonsai.

I took my first tree to my office at church. I placed it in a window with just the proper amount of sunlight. I watered it dutifully per the instructions on the little attached card on the "care and feeding of bonsai." All appeared to go well for the first several months. But alas, after these initial successful months, my bonsai began to drop needles and to show all the apparent signs of a sickness unto death. My diagnosis proved accurate and my thirty-dollar tree perished.

I was convinced that my secretary was the culprit in the untimely demise of my treasured tree. No doubt she had failed to water it faithfully while I was out of the office for a prolonged speaking engagement. You see, a bonsai requires daily watering since the root structure is so very small. The tiny, helpless victim was summarily pitched out without even a decent burial.

It wasn't long, however, until I owned another bonsai. My secretaries gave this one to me, proving my theory of neglect. A guilt gift, no doubt! This bonsai was accompanied by a fairly large pamphlet containing directions for growing a bonsai. Why should I bother with reading such obvious trivia? How hard could it be to keep a tree small and alive at the same time? I tossed my book into a drawer.

My new tree flourished for awhile, but then it too began to look sickly. Then I made a brilliant and well-calculated move. I read the bonsai pamphlet! If all else fails, read the instructions! I found this book fascinating. I soon bought another and then another bonsai book. When we traveled, I looked for bonsai at nurseries or in collections. With the aid of my trusty manuals, I soon began a collection of bonsai trees. Some I bought. Others I started from small seedlings. I had more than a dozen trees in my collection–a tiny tangerine that bore real fruit, several flowering trees, three different kinds of pines, and even a few hardwoods. These trees require a great deal of attention, but their miniature beauty never ceased to amaze me and visitors to our home.

One summer, two young ladies who were serving as summer interns at our church stayed in our home. One afternoon, they sat and watched me as I meticulously cared for my prized bonsai. They were astounded when I pulled one tree from its container, shook the dirt from the root ball, uncurled the roots, and began cutting them off.

"What are you doing?" they shrieked. "You'll kill it!"

Typical reaction of a novice! I assured them that I was not killing the tree; I was only making sure that it would remain small. This revelation created great interest.

"What else do you do to keep them small?"

I explained to them in great detail the secret behind the bonsai. The small pot, pruning the roots, and pinching back new growth were all critical to keeping the bonsai small and healthy. You can sound reasonably brilliant if you read the instructions!

Bonsai Churches

As we discussed the art of bonsai, *it dawned on me that the principles that keep a tree small will also keep a church small.* I know it sounds funny, but it's true. Most pastors and laymen that I talk to want their church to grow in a healthy manner. They want to reach their community for Christ. Yet, in spite of all their efforts to reach their community, their church remains the same size. *Why*, they wonder, *are we not growing?*

It is, in fact, the nature of a living organism to grow. All the biblical images of the church such as the body, the field, and the building presuppose a natural process of growth. It is my conviction that many churches, without knowing it, are doing things which virtually assure that they will remain small – a sort of bonsai church. If we can remove the actions that inhibit natural growth, the church should grow in a natural and proportionate manner.

IF WE CAN REMOVE THE ACTIONS THAT INHIBIT NATURAL GROWTH, THE CHURCH SHOULD GROW IN A NATURAL AND PROPORTIONATE MANNER.

It should be recognized from the beginning, that as there are numerous sizes of trees, there will be many sizes of churches. The giant redwood is not intrinsically better than the diminutive dogwood. Each tree is different, each has its own form, function, and beauty. This book is not about mega-churches. It does not presuppose that all churches should or could become very large churches. It does, however, suggest that a church, as a living organism, should grow to its natural, God-given size.

When Jesus established the church, as recorded in Matthew 16, *He promised He would build His church*. Thus, we can say that church growth is, at once, natural and supernatural. It is *supernatural* because God gives the growth and it is *natural* because the church was created as a living body to grow. The church must grow in such a manner that it fulfills the Great Commission beginning in its own community and extending to the ends of the earth (Acts 1:8). Yes, your church is designed to play a significant role in the fulfillment of the Great Commission. I have come to believe that church growth is natural and that artificial measures are being taken to keep a church from growing.

Are You Creating a Bonsai Church?

I would recommend that you consider the 40 day study entitled *Eternal Impact: The Passion of Kingdom-Centered Communities* to develop a biblical understanding of God's design and purpose for growing His church. The first issues of church growth for any church are ones of character. Methodological strategy must always be built on the foundation of character. Once God is allowed to change the character of your church, you can move ahead to deal with a contextualized strategy to enable your church to fulfill the Great Commission in its setting. Different churches will establish slightly differing strategies based on their context, their resources, and giftedness of their members.

Consider the following questions:

> 1. Are there factors in your church which have kept your church artificially small? What are they and what must you do to remove them?
>
> 2. Would you like to see your church be an effective Great Commission community?
>
> 3. Would you be willing to allow God to build His character in your church life?

If you can answer "yes" to these questions, you are ready to move forward as together we understand and remove the bonsai constraints that are keeping your church from living up to its potential.

1

KEEP THE POT SMALL

The bonsai pot may be the most identifiable accessory for growing bonsai trees. The pots come in numerous shapes and sizes. Some are very shallow, designed for planting a bonsai forest (several trees grouped together). Others are tall and somewhat narrow, used primarily for trees that cascade downward. Many look simply like miniature versions of more familiar flower pots. Most are ornate ceramic pots with Oriental-looking scenes and beautiful glazes. All of them are expensive when you consider their relative size. You might think that you wouldn't have to pay so dearly for such a small hunk of clay.

After only a cursory reading of my collection of bonsai books, I discovered that fitting the right pot to the right tree was an integral part of growing bonsai. The bonsai grower must take into account factors such as the size, shape, and color of the tree when making this crucial decision. In my case I added a fourth criterion – price.

Once the pot and the plant have been chosen, you're ready to go to work. The small tree must be placed in just the right position in the pot for the proper aesthetic beauty. Once this task has been completed you have embarked on your bonsai journey.

Yet the pot is much more than a simple decorative holder for a little tree. The pot in many ways helps to determine the size of the tree. The beautiful glazed dish must hold the dirt and roots that will support the tree's healthy growth. One of the secrets to the small size of the bonsai is the limited space for root growth.

This discovery about little trees applies to churches as well. The size of the container in which a congregation is planted will in many ways determine the size it will grow to in maturity.

We have seen this principle at work in the plants inside our home. Let's say, for example, that you purchase a small decorative fig tree from the local nursery. It comes to you in a one gallon container. You place your prized possession by an appropriate window and water it on a regular schedule and watch as it grows naturally for a year or so. We are surprised to see that it will grow with the virtual "benign neglect" that many of our plants receive. After about a year, you notice that the color of the leaves appears to be less vibrant and that some are actually falling from the tree. You continue to water your prized possession and even add a bit of fertilizer, but to no avail. What's the problem? It has become root-bound. The root structure has outgrown the one gallon container. The tree must be dug up, the roots untangled, and the tree repotted in a more spacious container if growth is to continue.

If the container can impede the growth of a perfectly healthy house plant, then the "church pot" can inhibit natural growth, even in a healthy church. Bonsai pots come in different shapes and sizes, but all are designed to keep the root structure of the plant small. In like manner, there are different "pots" your church must think about to promote healthy growth.

The Education Building

The most obvious container for the church is its building. Notice that the church and the building are not one and the same. The church is made up of people. It is a living, growing organism. The building is made of bricks, mortar, wood, and steel. It functions simply as a container for the church. The building is nothing more than a wrapper around ministry and cannot be allowed to restrict natural growth. Physical buildings can never be considered to be more important than the people they are designed to reach.

It took years of reading and practical experience before I could accept the fact that when any portion of the building is 80 percent filled, the church's natural growth will be inhibited and finally stopped. This rule-of-thumb can be applied to the worship center, an individual classroom, or the educational facility as a whole. Many churches have limited their growth because their facility restricts natural growth and development. Just as the container size affects the root ball of a bonsai, so the facility can restrict natural and healthy church growth. A church can be committed to growth, doing outreach, organizing people in small groups, and all the other right things and still not grow because the pot is too small.

If a classroom will accommodate 20 adults, the class occupying that room will grow to a size of about 16 persons in regular attendance. We arrive at that figure by applying the 80 percent saturation rule. A class or small group may actually over-crowd a room for a single high attendance emphasis, but they will not consistently maintain this saturation status. The class members may continue to aggressively enroll new persons, but the average attendance will remain static because the plant has become root-bound. In most instances small groups generally average about half of the enrollment in attendance on a given Sunday. But when a class continues to enroll people without adequate space for expansion, enrollment will continue to grow while the attendance remains the same. The small pot principle has had its effect.

If you want to promote healthy growth, you have several options. You can repot the class in a larger room, or you can create a new class by moving some of the members to an available classroom to start a new teaching unit. The second option is usually preferred because new units will allow you to maintain the small group dynamics of the class. It is also true that new units grow more quickly than older established units. Healthy churches strive to have 20 percent new units each year. That means that the church with 10 small groups should set a goal for 12 units the next year. The church with 20 will aim for 24 units etc. Each group should strive, with God's help, to give birth to a new class each year.

This limiting factor is more pronounced, but often ignored in preschool or children's rooms. Preschoolers and children require more floor space by the very nature of their educational needs. A particular church may have available rooms for new adult classes, but their preschool rooms are already overcrowded. Here, once again, the small-pot theory stifles the ability of this church to grow. If the preschool division or another similar division is unable to expand, the entire church's ability to grow will be restricted. Young couples are unlikely to join the church that does not provide adequate space for teaching their children.

If you would like to understand the different space requirements of preschoolers, children, youth and adults, I suggest that you read

Revitalizing the Sunday Morning Dinosaur. Chapter 9 of that book discusses the space needs of each age group. I would suggest the following guidelines to help you begin to assess your needs:

- Preschool – 20-35 square feet per child
- Children – 20-25 square feet per child
- Youth – 10-15 square feet per student
- Adult – 10 square feet per adult

Take the floor plan of your educational facility, utilize the 80 percent principle, and see where you have encountered bonsai pots. You can use the architectural drawing of your church for this project. It should have a scale which will enable you to determine the dimensions of each room. In the center of the room, indicate what age-group is meeting in the room. In the upper right corner, using the square footage requirements given above, write the maximum number of people the room will accommodate. Now using the 80percent rule, write the number at which saturation is reached in the bottom left corner. The total numbers in the left will tell you what your education building will actually accommodate.

In our rapid growth years at First Baptist, Norfolk, I often thought we could grow a big tree in a small pot. When I looked at the tremendous growth, it occasionally appeared that we had defied the 80 percent rule. Without warning, Sunday school growth stopped at an average of 1,700 persons in attendance. We continued to grow in worship because we had completed an addition to our worship center and had room to expand. We already had two Sunday school time frames and two worship services, but Sunday school attendance was static.

Upon close examination, we discovered we had no rooms in which to create new small groups. It is a basic truth that new groups grow more quickly. Thus our ability to grow had been limited by our container. We decided to begin a third Sunday school. About two hundred persons understood our dilemma and made the move to the early hour. In a matter of months, our small group attendance surged to over 1,900. By enlarging our space, we were able to accommodate new growth. A small pot artificially limits a tree from growing to its natural size. A small building can limit a church from growing to the natural size for reaching its community.

Many church families resign themselves to the small pot because they can't afford to build or land is not readily available. You can increase the size of your church without building. Consider off-site small groups. If there is a school or office building nearby, you can rent or borrow space. We had several single adult classes that met over the years in conference rooms at nearby hospitals and hotels and restaurants. Interestingly, some people attended these off-site classes who might never have come to the church building.

Off-site small groups might also meet in someone's home during the week. These home-groups can be attractive to persons who would not necessarily come to a church building. In the home environment, they can be introduced to the Christian journey and the teachings of Christ.

You can also have small groups meeting at several different time periods. This is one of the least expensive methods of enlarging your container. The building is already available and the cost of the additional utilities is minimal. When you use the same facility at several different time periods you will not have 100 percent more room because small groups for preschool and children's groups require more floor space and will often meet during the small group period and the worship time. You can usually count on adding approximately 70 percent more capacity.

In other words, if you discover that your existing building will hold 200 persons at its capacity, and you choose to use it twice for small groups, your 70 percent addition of space will allow you to grow to approximately 340 before you reach your new saturation point.

Multiple times for small groups and worship services provide many advantages and should be considered for both a short-term and a long-term pot enlargement idea. Not only does it provide "free" space, it also allows you to have worship services that differ in style. This has helped many churches to provide for the worship needs of various age groups. I know this seems like hard work, but it's worth the effort when we consider the demand of the Great Commission and the outreach potential created by new space.

Some people fear that utilizing several different times for worship and small groups will cause the church to sacrifice intimacy and fellowship. This is not the case. Fellowship is nurtured in the small groups and not created by the simple fact that people occupy a building at the same time. In truth, the addition of small groups will provide greater opportunity to experience genuine fellowship. Keep this in mind—biblical fellowship is never diluted by numerical growth. Fellowship can only be diluted by unconfessed and unforgiven sin (1 Jn. 1).

If you continue to reach your community, you will ultimately need to build additional space, employ multiple sites for small groups and worship, or participate in the planting of a new church. All of these are legitimate and should be viewed as a joyous opportunity for kingdom expansion and not as a necessary burden of church growth. The construction of buildings for the purpose of evangelistic outreach often serves to stimulate even more growth. The community interprets this as a sign of life. The people will see it as a commitment to fulfill the Great Commission. The same is true with the planting of a new church or employing several sites for Bible study. Life begets life!

However you choose to enlarge the container, enlarge it you must if you want to remove an artificial restriction to natural growth.

Worship Center

We must consider the worship center separately, since it is a separate container. The 80 percent principle impacts the worship center in the same way it affects the education space. When the worship center reaches 80 percent saturation, growth will slow, ultimately stop, and then decline begins. This creates what I call the *roller-coaster effect*.

A roller coaster slowly and steadily makes its way to the top of the first hill, providing the momentum to power it around the track. Once the coaster has reached the crest of the hill, the descent is considerably more rapid than the ascent. It then begins to move through a series of smaller hills and valleys, ultimately coming to a somewhat level plain. The roller coaster will not have sufficient momentum to again reach its highest peak after the initial drop.

We can illustrate the roller-coaster principle with a 200-seat sanctuary. Our congregation enters its new sanctuary with 100 persons in attendance. It has a steady process of growth until it reaches 160 in attendance. At this point, it has reached the bonsai saturation point. Notice that it can go beyond this point, but growth slows once attendance passes 160. It becomes increasingly more difficult to make progress as the 80 percent barrier is surpassed. This is caused by the crowded nature of the sanctuary.

Like the root-bound plant, the church roots have less space to expand. Most of us like a little extra space beside us in the pew and, therefore, we place our Bible or coat on the seat beside us. We also tend to sit near the end of the pew and the back of the church. We want to make sure that we are the first to the parking lot once the service is over. This seating pattern means that several gaps will remain in the center of most pews. Thus, it is exceedingly difficult to fill most churches to 100 percent of their seating capacity and maintain them at that level.

Obviously, if you are going to determine the saturation point of your sanctuary, you must first know how many it actually seats. There are three ways to determine this number, but two of them are unreliable. First, you can take the number suggested by the architect. This is usually 18 inches of pew space per person. I mean no offense to any individual in your church, but I've seen more than a few church members who might find the 18 inches a bit confining. In any case, we don't prefer to sit should-to-shoulder on a regular basis.

A second system of determining seating capacity is to base it on someone's "count" on a high attendance Sunday. These figures prove to be unrealistic. Since the desire was to "pack a pew," the church is often over-crowded for this one day. Often these counts are estimated on the high side. As time passes, our memory about such high attendance Sundays can become clouded. Perhaps your church once crowded 240 people into the sanctuary on an Easter Sunday that was accomplished by "shoe-spooning" 14 youth on one row. If the number lives on in the collective memory of the congregation as the capacity of our church, it can destroy realistic expectations and thus impede growth.

If your sanctuary has pews and not individual chairs, the most reliable way of determining its actual seating capacity is to have a group of adults seat themselves comfortably (not shoulder-to-shoulder) on a row and then multiply this number by the number of rows, less the first row. This process only works when your rows are of equal size. If they are different lengths, you must repeat the process on every row of a different size and then multiple by the number of rows of that specific length. If this seems a bit cumbersome, you will find 24 inches per person to provide a more realistic figure than the standard 18 inches suggested by the architect. After you find the capacity number, you will still need to take the 80 percent bonsai factor into consideration. When the attendance exceeds 80 percent, you are living on borrowed time. You can continue to grow in attendance, although growth will slow and finally stop. If additional space is not made available, decline will begin.

This may seem a bit mysterious to you, but if you have kept good attendance figures over the years, you will find that the numbers are accurate. Churches grow by momentum. When a church is growing, people are enthusiastic and thus they invite their friends. When decline begins, even if the decline is caused by the saturation of the building, people begin to wonder what is wrong with the church. Grumbling may begin. Declining momentum will actually pull the church further into decline. Because the roller coaster picks up speed on the downhill portions, this decline can be quite rapid. Often during these declining periods, the pastor and/or staff will become discouraged and leave the church. A declining church is much more difficult to pastor than a growing one because everyone wonders what is wrong.

In reality, many church buildings were constructed to hold 100 to 150 persons. In other words, their very design created a bonsai effect at around 80 to 120. This explains why 51 percent of churches average less than 100 attendees. With this limiting factor, many congregations and pastors are hesitant to plan multiple worship services for fear of losing community. Overcoming this mental model is a pre-requisite to launching sustained growth.

A church, committed to being an instrument God can use to fulfill the Great Commission, must be willing to provide adequate space for "root growth." If you can't afford to build a new sanctuary or education building or expand the existing one, you might want to consider two worship services or two Sunday schools. Using your space twice is good stewardship. Two services do not inhibit fellowship nor divide the church. Once a church has more than 35-40 active members, it has already passed the size where everyone will know everyone else. In any case, our goal is not to know everyone's name, but to faithfully reach everyone in the community.

Many churches are finding the multi-site approach to be advantageous when it comes to worship. You can have two worship services simultaneously on your own property if you have a fellowship hall or multi-purpose building. The equipment to send a live signal to a second site is relatively inexpensive today. Some churches choose to have live music (often different in style) in both locations and then have a video feed of the sermon. The same strategy can work for two or more separate locations. These multi-site locations may be the core for an eventual church plant. Use your God-given creativity, but do not allow lack of worship space to become a bonsai pot. (For more information on using multiple sites see *The Multi-Site Church Revolution* by Geoff Surratt, Greg Ligon, and Warren Bird.)

The Land

The acreage available for buildings and parking is another form of container. The church building and parking space must match the acreage. A good rule-of-thumb is that each acre will accommodate 100 people. If people have nowhere to park, you limit the number who will attend your church. I often encounter pious skeptics at this point. "If people really want to come to church they would be willing to walk!" That sounds good, but often those loudest in singing that refrain are the most unwilling to walk from a distant parking lot. But the larger issue is that most unsaved persons that the Great Commission church is attempting to reach won't walk across the street to visit your church.

You must provide adequate parking. Here again, our past memories may stand in the way of realistic present-day thinking. I once was presenting the bonsai material at a downtown church that had been much larger in the past. The pastor was feeling inadequate since he had been unable to lead the church to return to its level of former greatness. As I presented the case for the bonsai church, it was obvious that building space was not the bonsai pot that had prohibited growth. When I inquired as to the acreage owned by the church, I knew I had found the bonsai pot. It was the parking lot. Yet there were older members who argued that during the "glory days" the church had several hundred more people in attendance with the same size parking lot.

Their assessment was mistaken. Their glory days had been nearly 40 years prior to our conference. When I informed them that their parking lot had shrunk by nearly half its capacity, they were perplexed. I explained that 40 years ago, some families walked to church. Those families who drove had only one car. Today, many families arrive at church in two or three different vehicles. Thus, their parking lot would not accommodate as many people today as it would 40 years ago.

While I was pastor of First Baptist Norfolk, my family often required three cars to get us to church. I arrived early for my duties. My wife would drive a second car and my teenage daughter would insist on driving her own car. Forty years ago the church might anticipate four persons per car. Today most churches will find that they average only about 1.75 persons per car. You can see that most parking lots have actually shrunk by more than half in terms of capacity as we have become more prosperous.

You can discover the number of persons per car your church averages by counting the cars on Sunday and dividing that number into your attendance. You should probably count the cars during the small group hour and during worship for the most accurate assessment. If you have multiple times for small groups and worship, take a count during each session. For best results, take a count for several weeks and then average the numbers. Take your count about ten to fifteen minutes into the small group and worship times. Once you establish the average number of persons per car, multiply that by the number of parking spaces to determine the maximum capacity of your parking lot.

Example:
Attendance = 340
Cars 200 = 1.7 persons per car
Parking spaces available 220 X 1.7 = 374

The church in the example above has actually reached saturation in terms of parking since it is difficult to fill every spot with people arriving and departing at different times. It is not a bad rule-of-thumb to apply the 80 percent rule to your parking lot. Thus, in the example above, you would take 80 percent of the 374 and you will find that parking will become a "growth" issue at 299 persons in attendance. This does not mean that attendance will not exceed 299; it simply means that growth will slow after 80 percent is reached. If something is not done to alleviate the parking "bonsai pot," growth will stop.

Our church in Norfolk experienced problems with the parking lot. We did not have sufficient parking. It restricted growth. Were it not for a good number of folk who parked away from our church property, our growth would have stopped years earlier.

A few years into our growth, we instituted a preferred parking program. What, you might ask, is preferred parking? Let me illustrate by telling you where I got the idea. When I was being recruited to play football for a college team, I attended a game with an alumnus. Near the stadium, a guard spied a sticker on his car and waved him through the waiting traffic and parked him next to the gate right at the 50-yard line. That was my first experience with *preferred parking*.

It has been my experience, that in the Christian life, things are often opposite that of the world's standard. The first shall be last! The leader is the servant! Thus, our preferred parking allowed people to park off our church property. We took our cue from Romans 12:10, "Giving preference to one another in honor." We asked Christians to give up their space near the church in preference to those who need the on-site spaces – the elderly, the disabled, parents with small children, and the unsaved who are looking for a good excuse not to come to church.

The first priority would be to provide adequate on-site parking for expanded growth. If you cannot, you must use off-site parking. To reach newcomers, and particularly the unsaved, you should reserve the premium spaces for guests. Well-marked and easily accessible visitor places are essential for the church committed to reaching its community. Does your church have clearly marked spaces for guests? Are they near the entrance?

Churches should know how much land they have available when they are considering the addition of new buildings. It would not be wise to build a 1,000-seat sanctuary and appropriate education space on five acres of land. The church will have difficulty filling the new sanctuary because they won't have sufficient land to park the cars to fill the sanctuary. The philosophy "if you build it they will fill it" is only true if "they" can park when they arrive.

No matter which area you are addressing – education, worship center, or land – every congregation should have a master plan for their campus. Even if the church is not financially in a position to pay an architect to design a master plan, a vision planning team should document input from the congregation regarding the preferred future of the church campus. This plan, whether designed by an architect or a church team, should be flexible. The ability to build or expand based on the key growth area is more vital than simply building a space because it is the next item on the list.

Members of the congregation and the staff must leave personal preferences out of building plans. If anyone spearheads a building program that is self-serving and not based on growth need it can become an *emotional bonsai pot* which actually inhibits the growth of the church. I (Priest) served on staff at a church where the senior leadership decided to build a facility that was not meeting the key potential growth need of the congregation. The thinking was that building this particular building first was less expensive and would provide energy and momentum. In reality, this was counter-productive, though a nice addition to the campus. Though other factors have related to the present decline of this particular church, the congregational morale was low and the constructionof the un-necessary building was not strongly supported. Therefore, when the other factors presented themselves, the inevitable result was decline.

The Financial Pot

One critical pot many churches face in growth is the financial pot. One issue may be the church has grown to an 80 percent capacity point in one area and is making decisions regarding building or expanding facilities. Before reaching the 80 percent capacity point, establish a line-item for a building fund. This line-item can be expanded by individuals giving above and beyond their tithe. Also, if there are surplus funds at the end of the fiscal year, a portion may be allotted to this line-item.

Besides the financial concerns related to facility expansion in a growing church, ministry expansion also must be addressed by the finance team. Increases must be included for line-items such as curriculum and supplies, as well as the actual development and implementation of new ministry items not previously funded by the congregation. A growth process must be in place to address how the church will facilitate expanding and funding ministries, including leadership development. You might consider leading a stewardship study as a way of teaching healthy principles to resource utilization. *Making Change* is a tool available through Auxano Press and LifeWay Christian Resources which can provide this focus.

The idea that healthy growth will continue without adequate funding is wishful thinking. The bonsai pot of "stingy thinking" will quickly constrict growth. Think on adequate funding as the fertilizer that fuels healthy growth and kingdom advance. God is not asking your church to do anything He has not already provided the resources to accomplish. Read Paul's benediction in Ephesians 3: 20-21.

The Organization Pot

While the building, land, and budget may be the most obvious containers, they are not the only pots that can restrict growth. Your organization itself can restrict growth. If the organization of the church remains small, the ultimate size of the church will match the organization size.

For example, if you have four adult classes each averaging 12 persons, you will not grow appreciably from this figure of 48 adults in attendance until you enlarge the organization. You must add another class, or better, add two classes. The organization of the church is somewhat like the root system of a tree. If the organization remains small, the resulting tree will reflect the size of the organization.

Many churches have practiced this principle of church growth through expanding the organization without realizing it. Let's take a church that has been averaging about 100 in small group Bible study for years. One day, two young married couples come to the pastor and ask if they can start a new class for young couples. The class is started with the two couples who quickly invite other couples in the community who were not previously attending church. At the end of the year, the pastor notices that the average attendance is now 112. What happened? The organization was expanded and growth followed.

The pyramid principle of church growth visualizes growth on the basis of the construction of a pyramid. The size at the base of a pyramid will ultimately determine the height the pyramid will reach. The base of the church growth pyramid is determined by the number of small groups in the Bible study organization. If you desire to allow the Bible study attendance of your church to grow naturally, you must continue to add new Bible study units to the organizational base. This will allow the Bible study organization to accommodate the new people who are being reached.

You may be wondering, *what is the ideal size for an adult small group unit or Sunday school class?* Most church growth experts point to *attendance* figures ranging from 12 to 15 with an enrollment of 25 to 30. Some unique situations enable classes to grow beyond this size, but the crucial factor is the organizational structure of the class for ministry. When a class becomes too large, it often fails to care adequately for the relational needs of its members.

We teach the principle of multiplying small groups and champion the cause for appropriate organizational structure. However, we have discovered that everyone doesn't listen. After serving on staff for over ten years, I (Priest) have now had the opportunity to go back on the "normal church member" side of ministry and attend small groups at several different churches.

As Debbi and I have attended churches for the past couple years, and been part of Bible Fellowship Groups, we have seen how the lack of organization directly impacts the potential growth of the class. The critical issue is found in the ability of the class to care for members. One class we know did a great job of connecting with new members; however, the same effort was not put into caring for existing members. The mind-set was, "they're members, they should want to be here and attend more often, then we wouldn't have to reach out to them." While it is true that members should attend regularly, there may be times when this becomes problematic. We have seen that when persons encounter a crisis in their life, whether spiritual or physical, they respond in one of two ways. Either they grow closer to God through the crisis, partly due to the church small group responding in a healthy way; or they grow farther from God, due in part to ineffective care ministry during the crisis. We hear comments such as, "they don't care about me" and "no one was there for us."

1 to 8 Principle of New Units

Churches may have high-attendance Sundays or special events and greatly improve attendance for a short time. However, attendance gradually drops back to its *normal level* unless the organization itself is expanded to provide for a larger tree. This organization pot cannot be overlooked if you desire to reach your community for Christ.

A healthy approach is to employ the *1 to 8 Principle*. One new small group should be started for every eight existing small groups every year. This is essentially 12 percent growth per year in small group expansion. Historically, an evangelistically focused new unit will enroll twenty or more persons in the first year of existence. Most churches will average 50 percent of enrollment in attendance. Therefore, each new unit with an enrollment of twenty will be expected to have an average attendance of ten persons. This *1 to 8 Principle* also applies to the Leadership Pot.

The Leadership Pot

The organization itself cannot be enlarged, unless the leadership pool is enlarged. The growing church must have sufficient numbers of well-trained and committed leaders if it is to continue to grow in a natural and healthy fashion. Some people believe this is actually the key principle of church growth. It is certainly critical. Little can be done to expand the organization without sufficient leadership to staff the enlarged organization.

1 to 8 Principle of Leadership

As mentioned in the previous section, the *1 to 8 Principle* applies to leadership as well. Different authors may use slightly different numbers to discuss the need for expanding the leadership pot, but all agree it must be done. Andy Anderson in his 1993 B&H book *The Growth Spiral* argues for a 1 to 5 leadership rule; others say 1 to 10. I (Priest) believe a middle ground is the place to be. The concept is for every eight members there should be one leader in your small group structure. Following this principle will enable you to connect persons to the church through meaningful service. Jeri Herring and Larry Garner point out in their material, *Five Handles for Getting a Grip on Your Sunday School*, "If members are to stay active, they must have some job of meaningful service within three to six months." Here's the good news– Involving people in leadership positions increases the size of your leadership pot and stops people from leaving the church through the back door.

Many churches overlook the need for growing the leadership pot by not providing for sufficient professional staff members. The professional staff is responsible for equipping the saints for the work of ministry. Most church-growth leaders recommend one professional staff person per 150 to 200 people involved in small groups. If the leadership structure breaks down at this most basic level, little can be accomplished in recruiting and training sufficient lay leadership. The church committed to growth will have to ensure that the leadership pot is continually enlarged.

The church must plan ahead and provide adequate budget to call additional staff persons. Often a growing church will need to call an individual who will share two responsibilities, such as music and youth, youth and education, or some other combination. This may be wise during these early growth years. Every staff person will have multiple tasks. As the church grows, greater specialization is preferable. Most staff persons who are in a combination position are stronger in one area than the other. Allow them to serve in that area and bring someone else on board to do the others tasks.

Every member of the church staff should be involved in evangelistic outreach whatever their job description. A primary function of the professional ministerial staff is to equip lay persons for the work of ministry. A growing professional staff does not mean that fewer laypersons will be required. The entire organizational structure—lay and professional—must grow in a balanced manner. However, a growing staff does require a commitment on the part of the church to call and compensate staff sufficient for growth.

If we are going to enlarge the leadership pot, a majority of staff time must be spent equipping lay leaders. This is the biblical picture painted by the apostle Paul in Ephesians 4:11-16. Every growing church will *always* face the need for more leadership. This need should never deter you from reaching your community for Christ.

At the end of Matthew 9, Jesus declared that the fields are ripe unto harvest. The limiting factor, Jesus pointed out, was the lack of laborers. Jesus then did two things. First, He exhorted the disciples to pray for sufficient laborers. Few churches spend adequate time praying for laborers before they actually seek them out. Prayer is the key to all church growth.

The second thing Jesus did was to send His disciples on a missionary journey to seek lost persons. We may be surprised that Jesus sends the disciples to gather more persons immediately after decrying the lack of laborers. Many churches become paralyzed when they don't have sufficient leadership. They think, *Why should we do outreach? We don't care for the persons we have now.* They stop reaching out, and then they stop growing because they lose their focus on the Great Commission. This accounts for the thousands of churches that have grown and then plateaued. Follow Jesus' example. Pray and reach out.

A great tool for expanding your *leadership pot* is to help your members to discover their spiritual gifts and then implement a process such as *PLACE*. Dr. Hemphill's study *You Are Gifted* provides a biblical basis for gifted ministry while the PLACE process assists churches with assimilation by helping members discover how God has uniquely created and gifted them for service within the context of their present congregation.

As I (Priest) have worked with churches over the past fifteen years, I have learned that the discovery of spiritual gifts is a critical issue for the growing church. Teaching about spiritual gifts and encouraging persons to serve is not enough in our present culture. I worked in the hospitality, theme-park industry prior to seminary and ministry. One definite life-lesson stood out -- no matter how much signage is available, people have to be clearly directed to find their way.

Pastors and staff must communicate more than the simple message that everyone is gifted and should use his/her gift in service. They must become more intentional in illustrating the *how-to's* of service. It is not enough to parade the babies through the worship center and say, "Some of you should serve in the nursery." Working with preschool, children, students, or adults is a definite calling. This is the great benefit of a process such as *PLACE*. Their process involves creating a ministry catalog. This process will also help you to consider what future volunteer opportunities might be available as the church continues to grow.

PLACE engages the entire process of personality assessment, spiritual giftedness, abilities awareness, passions, and life experiences. This approach insures that persons not only know how God has created them, but specifically how they can fulfill their purpose for being within the church at this particular time in history.

The Vision Pot

In many situations the most confining pot may be that of vision. Churches often fail to see and seize the opportunities for growth right in front of them. The early disciples were sometimes guilty of restricted vision. In John 4, Jesus instructed the disciples to lift up their eyes and look on the fields for they were ripe for the harvest. The disciples were unable to see this opportunity for growth. They were, at that moment, in Samaria. The long-standing animosity between the Jews and the Samaritans had restricted the vision of the disciples.

Small vision hampers church growth. A church may have small vision because of class or racial barriers like those of the disciples. They assume that "those" people would not want to worship with us (or maybe, we don't want "them" worshipping with us). We often fail to consider their needs. Vision can be limited by the lack of space, land, money, resources, or leadership. We can find ourselves in a never-ending cycle of negativity.

I have had the opportunity to share growth principles in conferences across the country. I find it fascinating that in almost every situation, I hear pastors and laypersons decrying the fact that their location is the most difficult location for growing a church. It appears that everyone finds their soil unsuitable for church growth! Because of this lack of vision, many churches languish in a bonsai condition. In each of these locations, I have also encountered pastors and people who see unlimited potential. In most cases someone else is growing a great church; therefore, they see that it can be done. In others, they see the absence of a great church as a golden opportunity. They exclaim, "No one is doing it here; the opportunities are absolutely unlimited." What a difference vision makes!

A church will never have sufficient resources for growth until it catches a great vision for reaching its community. The vision must come first. Many believers and churches fail to reach their full potential because they do not understand the crucial role of vision. Before the church will grow in a natural manner, there must be a thorough understanding of the biblical foundations of the church. If you are desire a study on the biblical characteristics of the church, you may want to consider the 40 day study *Eternal Impact: The Passion of Kingdom-Centered Communities.*

When Jesus first spoke of the church in Matthew 16, He declared that He would build His church. We must understand that the church has a divine origin and a supernatural empowering. It is His intention to empower His church to grow naturally, enabling it to fulfill the Great Commission in its setting.

The vision must begin in the heart of the pastor before it penetrates the church. Once the pastor catches God's vision for the church, he must boldly share it with the congregation. He must preach, teach, and encourage others to catch a glimpse of the supernatural empowering of the church. Once a majority of the leaders and members of the church catch a vision of the church unleashed, they will discover solutions for the problems that cause the church to struggle.

Jesus promised His disciples that *He would build His church* (Matt. 16:18). That's a supernatural promise that will not return void. You can, however, restrict that growth by a pot which artificially limits the natural process of supernatural church growth. "Where there is no vision, the people perish" (Prov. 29:18, KJV).

FERTILE THOUGHTS AND ACTIONS

1. The building can limit your church's ability to grow. What is the maximum size of your small group and worship facilities based upon the 80 percent full principle?

2. What possibilities exist for off-site small group Bible study classes?

3. Do acreage and parking inhibit your church's growth? What can be done to expand your land and parking potential?

4. Effective organization is based upon the ability of the church to create new units. How many existing units in your small group Bible study are over their maximum enrollment and attendance numbers for effective ministry? How many new units need to be created in order for your church to experience growth?

5. The ability of any church to grow largely depends upon its ability to enlist new leaders. There should be at least one worker for every eight persons enrolled in small group Bible study. What is the worker/member ratio in your small group structure?

6. What is your vision for your church? Imagine what your church will look like three years from now. What do you see? How will it be different? How will you help these changes to occur?

7. What is your vision for your own personal growth as a small group or church leader? Are you growing so that your small group and church can continue to grow also? Develop an outline for your personal growth for the next year. What will you read? What conferences will you attend? Who will you invite to your church, so that you and your church can hear from other growth experiences?

PRUNE THE ROOTS

The most difficult bonsai technique for me to accept was the annual or biannual pruning of the roots. You heard right! On a regular basis you must remove the bonsai from its container, comb the dirt away from the root structure, and prune the roots. Because of the limited size of the bonsai container, the bonsai can easily become root-bound. The small size of the container limits the tree's ability to gather life-giving nutrients; therefore, it is essential that the roots be maintained at a suitable size for the container.

The first time I performed this task I knew I had killed my prized tree. Theoretically, I understood that pruning the roots was essential if I was going to keep my tree small. I had one particularly beautiful bonsai with lovely white blooms. I had let it grow for three years without pruning the roots. I began to notice an appreciable difference in the number of blooms on the tree. A friend, more established in the art of growing small trees, diagnosed the problem – root-bound – the roots must be cut back. I panicked! *I can't do it!*

With fear and trepidation, I performed the mandatory root pruning with the tenderness of a surgeon. To my surprise my tree didn't die. It is, nonetheless, the most traumatic time in the life of the bonsai and its owner. The tree is placed at risk during the time of root pruning.

Yes, indeed, churches prune roots to keep themselves small. Often, they do it without understanding that they are involved in root pruning, or that this process will ensure that their church will remain small. Let's look at a few examples of how root pruning can produce a bonsai church!

Enrollment Pruning

Many churches go through an annual root pruning by lopping off persons who are on the roll but have not attended during the last year. It is difficult to determine how this process came to be so prevalent in many churches. I suspect it came about because someone wanted to know what percentage of the membership attended on a particular Sunday. Many small groups take great pride in having 100 percent of their enrollment in attendance. This is really not a difficult goal to accomplish. You need merely to trim off all those people who do not attend regularly.

Don't misunderstand me; we should be concerned about those people on our church rolls who are inactive or sporadic. The best way to deal with these cumbersome *extra roots*, however, is not to cut them off, but to seek them out and restore them to fellowship. When a church prunes what appears to be "dead" roots, they will often damage healthy roots. In other words, friends and family members of those purged from the rolls can be offended and leave the church.

Our primary goal is not to boast about the percentage of members present, but to reach the unsaved in our community and to care for the inactive in our fellowship. We're not caring for someone when we prune them from our rolls. We simply lose contact and opportunity for ministry. The church that goes through the annual process of root pruning will invariably remain small. Our small group enrollment is not maintained for the pride of the church, but for the progress of the kingdom.

A few years ago, I went to California to lead several Sunday school growth conferences. I arrived in San Francisco late on Sunday evening. My host insisted that we do a little sightseeing. To my surprise, San Francisco was very much alive late at night. He suggested that we make a final stop at a well-known chocolate factory for a hot fudge sundae. Just what I needed to put me to sleep! On our way, we passed the building of a famous mail-order catalog business.

I recognized the name because I had ordered a pants-press from them. The object arrived promptly as advertised. In the weeks following, an interesting process began. I received, almost daily, full-color catalogs from nearly every mail-order business in the United States. My wife wanted to know why I had ordered all those catalogs. They create quite a temptation with three daughters in the house. I quickly denied guilt. "I didn't do it." We realized what had happened. The mail-order company, from which I had ordered the pants-press, sold my name to other mail-order companies.

I thought about the difference between churches who prune away prospects and businesses that pay money for them. When we understand that the people on our rolls are persons for whom Jesus died, we will treasure any and every contact with them. When we prune them from our roll, we forfeit opportunities to touch their lives for the kingdom of God. Don't prune them; go find them.

There are only two ways anyone should be removed from the roll. If the individual joins another evangelical church in your community and becomes active in that fellowship, you should remove them from the roll. When people move from your community, you should make every attempt to help them locate a new church fellowship in their new community. When someone goes home to be with the Lord, we can assume they are enjoying wonderful fellowship in heaven.

Yes, people occasionally want to be removed from the church roll, although they do not yet meet the prescribed conditions. Those calls or requests should be routed to the pastor or someone designated to handle such requests. Often the individual will be going through a difficult period and therefore are in need of care.

While I was a pastor, I would occasionally get calls from persons who indicated a desire to be removed from the roll, but what they actually wanted was to stop receiving mail outs from the church, especially offering envelopes. If this occurs, you can readily agree to discontinue sending those items. You should, however, decline to remove their names from the roll. Tell these persons that you care for them and that the church family cares for them. Therefore, you will retain their name in order to be available for ministry when needed. Be prepared to follow through on this commitment. You will almost always have the opportunity.

The policy of not dropping names from the roll has proved beneficial to our ministry. There have been occasions when a family has called our church during a time of bereavement. The surviving children may call, needing our help. Because the church has kept the rolls intact and maintained those names, we have a new opportunity to minister to the family during a teachable moment.

On one specific occasion, we discovered two persons from our young married department who could easily have been pruned from the roll years earlier. Our church had a bus ministry in the past. Many of those children had not attended in years, yet their names remained on roll. When we renewed and improved our process for keeping in contact with our members, we called one young lady. We discovered she had subsequently married and was quite interested in returning to our church.

I'm not suggesting that anyone should retain names for the sake of padding the enrollment numbers. Church growth is not about numbers, but about people. I do, however, recommend that every effort be made to stay in contact with everyone God gives us in our sphere of influence. Keep the rolls intact and updated. A name on the church or small group roll is an open invitation to ministry.

The roll is best kept updated by regular contact. A card or an occasional phone call can make a vast difference in the church's ministry. The person may not immediately respond, but the person making the contact receives joy and blessings that carry over to the Sunday school class and church.

You should develop some system for contacting everyone in the church and small group rolls on a regular and consistent basis. I have found that having care leaders in every small group is the most efficient and effective way to accomplish this task. Each care leader should have no more than four persons or families to contact. The care leader should call each person each week to discover if there are any needs that the church should be made aware of. Each call should end with prayer for the individual. (For more information for establishing and maintaining a care ministry through small groups see Ken Hemphill's, *Revitalizing the Sunday Morning Dinosaur,* chapter 7).

Combining Classes

How often have you seen churches combine two classes to make one large one? This is a subtle way of pruning roots, but the outcome is essentially the same. The organization of the Sunday school is cut back, and this pruning process will inevitably lead to a smaller tree. Combining two classes absolves the leaders from equipping enough competent teachers, and it absolves the classes from reaching out to the community to ensure growth.

Combining classes is opposite of what needs to be done for natural growth. The healthy church will always be looking to start new units. I do not like to see classes combined even for a week or so during the summer. The temporary combining of classes inhibits natural growth, reduces opportunities for service, and disrupts the care ministry of the church. Enlist a substitute and keep the class structure intact. These vacation periods may actually provide a wonderful opportunity to train and enlist future teachers and care leaders.

Cutting Back Resources and Money

Every church hits the occasional financial slump. It may occur during a building project or a down time in the local economy. When it occurs, there is a temptation to cut back in the resources available for ministry. This is a self-defeating move. Pruning the financial roots in terms of providing the resources for Bible study, leadership development, and the like ultimately leads to slower growth or actual decline. This, in turn, creates greater financial difficulties. Financial pruning can cause the beginning of a death spiral.

I am aware that financial challenges are not easy to resolve. But in the times of financial slowdown, every effort should be given to provide the resources for accomplishing the tasks which enable the church to fulfill the Great Commission. It may require cost-cutting in other nonessential budget areas. Financial challenges should be met with courage and seen as an opportunity to teach the principles of biblical stewardship. Establish regular times of prayer and fasting that are focused on seeking God's face and turning from our own selfish agendas. This could provide the platform for genuine revival in your church.

When stewardship training is tied together with the vision for fulfilling the Great Commission, it has its most positive results. Church members can be led to understand that God allows us to be the stewards of His resources precisely so that we can join Him in advancing His kingdom. The budget of every church should be seen as a blueprint that enables the church to fulfill the Great Commission and thus advance God's kingdom. Giving is not a duty but the privilege of Kingdom people. Persons who serve on the financial teams of the church should be selected because they have a passionate desire to see the church accomplish its mission. They must understand basic church growth principles and be committed to the mission and vision of the church.

Pruning the financial roots will greatly hamper the natural growth of the church. God has promised to provide all the resources necessary to accomplish the task He has given us.

Staff Only Ministry

A few forms of root-pruning are not as obvious as those listed above. For example, the congregation that expects the pastor or staff to perform all ministry functions, practices subtle but sure "root-pruning." This root-pruning technique cuts back the effective caring ability of the church and thus restrains natural growth. When a church restricts ministry to the ordained staff, it will ensure that the church remains at a significantly reduced size. More importantly, it follows a non-biblical pattern that limits caring ministry to the "professional" staff. This will have a further negative impact of keeping God's gifted people from experiencing the joy of serving God through their spiritual gifts.

In Ephesians 4:11-12, Paul speaks of the pastors/teaches whom God has given to the church to equip the saints (believers) to do the work of ministry. In that same context, He speaks of the church growing up into its Head (Christ) through the proper functioning of each individual part (4:15-16). If you are interested in learning more about the functioning of the gifted members, you might enjoy my 12 week study entitled *You Are Gifted: Your Gifts and the Kingdom of God.*

Lack of Guests

You can also accomplish an unintentional root-pruning if you do not have a sufficient number of guests to challenge your outreach ministry. You should have at least one "potential believer" for every person enrolled in your Bible study program to provide a sufficient root system to allow for sustained growth. You can find "potential believers" by asking every church member to provide the names of friends or relatives who do not have a church home. Once you have the names, begin to pray that God will work in their lives to make them susceptible to the gospel. The final step is to visit them in their homes and invite them to come to small group events.

The most effective marketing plan any church can develop is "word of mouth." Church growth studies confirm that a majority of persons select a particular church because they were invited by a friend or family member. Further, they indicate that most "potential believers" would attend church next Sunday if taken by a friend.

Pruning the roots serves the bonsai well, but it hurts the growing church. God never intended for us to have cute churches that remain artificially small. He desires for us to have healthy churches that effectively reach their communities.

⊘ FERTILE THOUGHTS AND ACTIONS

1. What is the enrollment philosophy of your small groups and church? How and why are people removed from the rolls?

2. How many persons have been enrolled in your small groups in the past two years? How many have been unnecessarily removed through root pruning?

3. Are there ministries of your church being severely hindered by lack of funds? List these.

4. Is there a plan for increasing giving that is clearly understood by the congregation?

5. What can you do to help others in your church to understand the negative impact of the pruning principle?

3

PINCH OFF THE NEW GROWTH

One of the more curious tasks the bonsai grower must do on a regular basis is to pinch off new growth. This is particularly true with little pine trees. It's quite easy to tell new growth from the old by the color alone. The new growth is light green and appears at the ends of the branches. It is a lovely, refreshing sign that the tree is healthy and growing. Thus, it was difficult for me to bring myself to pinch this sure sign of new growth off my trees. But the books assured me that it was essential that this new growth be twisted off in order to keep the tree small.

You've noticed the words *pinching* and *twisted off*. These words should be taken literally. The new growth is so tender; you need no tool to remove it. A simple twist is sufficient. The pinching method doesn't leave the scar that pruning might.

Here, once again the parallels with church practices beg for comment. Most churches do not go about the task of inhibiting "new" growth in an intentional manner as I do with my bonsai, but the results are surely the same. Pinching off new members is much more subtle than pruning roots but it is equally effective if you want to keep your church artificially small.

Pinching Off the New Members

New members join your church and are full of excitement and joy. They are oblivious to all the flaws and imperfections of their new church home. They bask in the exhilaration of their new-found community. Now, while they're still green, is the time we often pinch off this immature enthusiasm.

We pinch them off by refusing to allow them to become involved in the ongoing structure and life of the church. We want people to prove themselves before they are deemed worthy of service or leadership. In some churches, anyone who hasn't lived in the community for 25 years is a "newcomer." Ever hear comments like these? "We can't let these newcomers serve as care leaders or small group leaders. We don't know what they're like." This sort of attitude pinches off new growth.

If the newcomers are new believers, we would do them a disservice by putting them in places of spiritual leadership before they are prepared. This would be dangerous for them and detrimental to the life of the church. We must assist our new members in the discovery and use of their spiritual gifts. In so doing, we will help them to become involved in the church and to grow in their spiritual commitment. You might find the training material mentioned in the last chapter *(You Are Gifted)* to be a helpful tool for involving new members in service.

There are, however, several things we should encourage new members to begin doing in the life of the church. Without hesitation, you should take new Christians with you as you visit other class members. You should offer to join them as they tell friends or relatives about their relationship to Christ. Such visits will often prove to be fruitful evangelistic opportunities. You can also allow new members to plan or host a fellowship event for the class. Involve your new members on a team or service group in the church. If they have musical abilities, you can incorporate them into the music program of the church. Involve them quickly or you will surely pinch them off.

In *Five Handles for Getting a Grip on Your Sunday School* authors Jeri Herring and John Garner cite North American Mission Board research that states, "If members are to stay active, they must begin a relationship in a small group within one month AND must be involved in meaningful service within three to six months." This research demonstrates the need to insure we do not pinch off new growth.

In other instances, those who join our churches have been growing Christians for many years. They may have moved to our community from another state and felt led to join our church. Often these persons bring in fresh ideas from their own experience. All too often, churches impose some artificial waiting period that must be endured before these persons can serve in their new church home. We must come to the realization that God brings mature believers into the congregation in His timing to provide mature, ministry-minded persons at critical moments in the life of the church. By creating artificial limitations on how long someone has to be a member prior to serving, we limit God's work in having them present for such a time as this. At other times, we pinch new members back by turning a deaf ear to their new ideas. When we pinch back new growth, we ensure that the tree will remain small.

We pinch back new growth when we expect our new members to find a place of service without some specific plan, approach, or program for helping them. We often assume new members will find their class and their place of service on their own. The first few weeks, in a new church family, is a crucial time for involving new members. Follow-up must be immediate, specific, and organized or you will pinch back new growth. This is one of the most important, but also most difficult tasks of the growing church. It is one thing to get members to do evangelistic outreach and quite another to get them to do adequate in-home follow-up.

Some new members have candidly told me that they felt like they were being courted when they were visiting the church. Once they joined, the only follow-up contact came in the form of offering envelopes and a form letter welcoming them to the church. Now that's effectively pinching off new growth.

Every new member should be personally enlisted and enrolled in a small group Bible study. Your church may attract people through the worship service, but you will not keep them involved if they do not get involved in a small group. Involvement in small-group Bible study cannot be seen as an option. You cannot coerce attendance, but you can establish a pattern that makes small-group Bible study involvement a normal expectation.

Take these three steps and you will have good results: (1) enroll all new members in the appropriate small group, (2) visit each person in their home to explain the virtue of the small-group experience, and (3) personally bring them to class with you. The easiest way to organize your small-group program for outreach and assimilation is to grade it by age. You can find an effective strategy for assimilation through small groups in my book, *Revitalizing the Sunday Morning Dinosaur.*

Pinching Off with Tradition

"We don't do things that way here!" Sounds like a refrain from a familiar hymn. New members bring new ideas. Some may sound unorthodox. Some may be unorthodox! But *not all new ideas are bad!* One of the surest ways to pinch off new growth is to douse the enthusiasm of a new idea.

I must confess that, as a pastor, I was sometimes guilty of this. There were times that a layperson would come to me with a novel solution for a problem. My first reaction was to think: *What does this guy think he's doing — trying to tell me how to do my job. I'm the expert here!* We may not think in just those terms, but when we reject the new or novel suggestion, we pinch off the enthusiasm of new growth. We must be open to that new idea; it may well be the moving of God's Spirit. God can, after all, speak through new ideas and new members if He so chooses.

Shut Them Out of Class

Rarely does a group of Christians determine that they will isolate or ostracize the new member. No, it's much more subtle than that. They can do the same pinching back if they just ignore the new-comer. If newcomers to your church do not make new friends and find fellowship in the first few months, they will probably become a "back-door" statistic. Nobody really wants it to happen. Yet we are quite ready to say: "Those newcomers just aren't committed like we are. They don't understand all the hard work we've done to build our church. They never last long around here." No wonder! It's hard to last when the attitude of the church or class is always twisting you off. Remember that new growth occurs on tender young shoots.

The process of shutting newcomers off from fellowship frequently occurs in churches where the small group structure is not age-graded. Thus, there is no adult promotion and the adult classes tend to stagnate. Newcomers threaten the "fellowship" (in truth, "coziness" would be a more accurate word) of the class. New members are never truly accepted into the life of that class and thus they quite expectedly "fall away."

The tragedy with the pinching off technique is that it crushes the enthusiasm of new Christians and other newcomers. Often permanent damage is done. If you have ever talked to the person who has been pinched off by another church, you know what I mean. They've been hurt by the rejection and they're reluctant to join another church and risk being hurt again.

Pinching off new members is often defended by a rather syrupy spirituality, "These new folks never last. They're not willing to pay their dues." I thought Christ paid all the dues. Don't we all walk on level ground at the foot of the cross? Does the Bible not teach that the last shall be first?

Our goal should be that every member is seen as vital to Christ and to His body, the church.

Ignoring Friends

We frequently pinch back evangelistic growth opportunities when we fail to ask new Christians to identify other non-Christian family members and friends. When people experience new birth, they are usually enthusiastic to share their new-found relationship with others. These new Christians are unsure and ill-equipped to share their faith with an unsaved friend.

We must give encouragement by offering to go with them to visit friends or family members. Send someone who can present the gospel and ask the new Christians to share their own personal testimony. This must be done immediately since new Christians will frequently forfeit these friendships soon after conversion. Their "old friends" are often dismayed that their "former" friends no longer want to do the same things they used to do together. Yet the difference in interests and life-style can provide an effective illustration for sharing the gospel.

Restrictive Enrollment

Some churches insist that people prove themselves before they can be enrolled in the Sunday school or small-group organization of the church. "You must attend three times to be a member here." The intentions may be well meant, but the effect is often detrimental to evangelistic growth. The growing church will practice an open enrollment policy. This does not mean that you should lower the standards for becoming a part of your church. (The only biblical standard for church membership is a born-again relationship with Christ.) Yet, there should be a small-group organization in your church that people are encouraged to join without any restriction. Unsaved people enrolled and nurtured through small-group Bible study units will frequently accept Christ within the first year. Don't pinch away those fragile shoots.

Pinching Back Through Lack of Affirmation

A lack of affirmation and encouragement of both new and present members pinches back new spiritual growth. Recognize and acknowledge spiritual breakthroughs in life. The church often expects a great deal in terms of service and giving without providing the "thank you" and biblical affirmation which must occur to ensure that new growth remains. Every healthy church needs both formal and informal methods of affirming new members and the spiritual growth and service of all church members.

Some of the most neglected phrases in the church today are:"Thank you; I appreciate you; Good job; We care; You are loved; How are you doing? and, May I help?" These questions and affirmations must be genuine and heartfelt. They must be a constant if we are to ensure that new growth is not pinched off by discouragement and disillusionment. You can also schedule regular events where the church says "thank you" to members for giving, serving, and going.

The green growth at the end of the limb is the sign of life. Don't pinch it back.

 **FERTILE THOUGHTS AND ACTIONS**

1. What is the written or unwritten requirement for new members before they are asked to serve in your congregation?

2. List some traditions that keep your church from growing and reaching its full potential.

3. How healthy is the friendship network in your church? Take a brief survey of members to find out.

4. What program do you have for involving and training new members?

4

SOIL IS BASIC

Soil may well be the most critical element in growing a bonsai tree. The small pot contains such a small quantity of soil, it cannot be overlooked. The soil allows the roots to get sufficient moisture. If the soil doesn't drain well, the roots will rot. If it drains too quickly, the tree will experience drought.

You can buy premixed bonsai soil from most nurseries, or you can make your own. To make your own, mix sand, peat moss, and earth in equal proportions. Mix all ingredients together using a shovel or garden trowel, depending on the amount needed. Since each tree receives only a small quantity of soil, it is important not to have chunks of clay or rock. Some bonsai trees – conifers, for example – do better in slightly drier soil. For those trees you should add two parts sand. This will allow for faster drainage. For broad-leafed trees you can use two parts earth which will retain water longer. As you learn more about bonsai, you come to understand the complexities of soil textures.

In our comparison of the church and the bonsai, what can we learn from the soil?

Understanding the Soil

The bonsai pot contains a small amount of soil, and because the soil is essential to healthy growth, knowledge of the soil is critical. Many churches fail to grow because they do not understand the nature of the soil in their community. The Lord taught the disciples about the importance of understanding the soil when He sent them into the fields ripe for harvest (Matt. 10). He indicated that some soils would be more receptive to the seed of the gospel than other forms of soil. Nonetheless, the faithful planter must continue to sow. We must never let the condition of the soil become an excuse for the bonsai condition of our church.

Through prayer and with the aid of the Holy Spirit, we can change the condition of the soil. Before we can change it, we must first understand it.

What do you know about your soil? What do you know about the community around your church? Church members and pastors alike are often surprised to discover how little they do know. Give yourself a simple test.

1. What is the population of your community?
2. What are the age breakdowns within that population?
3. How many students attend the local elementary school(s)? Middle school(s)? High school(s)?
4. What special needs exist in your neighborhood? (Disabled persons, low income, single parents, etc.)

How well did you do?

Taking a Soil Sample

As you can see from our little test, the first essential bit of information is basic demographic facts. Who lives in your church community? How old are they? What is their educational background? What physical and emotional needs do they have? For example, an aging community will require more first-floor space and disabled facilities for senior adults. A community with a high concentration of young adults will require adequate facilities for preschool and school-age children.

The answer to these and other questions should determine the organizational structure of your church, as well as the allocation and use of space. These facts should help you decide what additional staffing and programming you may need to add, in order to meet the needs of your community. Many churches do not take a soil sample to determine their outreach approach to their community. Since the soil and the tree must be compatible, a failure to understand our soil will almost assuredly cause the church to remain in a bonsai condition, or worse yet, to die.

Drive-Through Survey

If you are wondering how to get started in collecting a soil sample, let me make a few suggestions. A first step might be a simple walk-through or drive-through of your community. Much can be determined by careful observation. Look for telltale clues such as swing sets, bikes, or wheelchair ramps to alert you to the makeup of your community. (See www.auxanopress.com for some free tools to help with this).

Check Other Sources

Much of the demographic information is available through www.census.gov. Call your local city or county information center to inquire about additional information concerning your community. (Southern Baptist churches can request help in determining their soil conditions from Southern Baptist state conventions or your local associational office). No doubt, other denominations offer similar help to their churches. Just Ask.

Needs Survey

One of the most effective, but often overlooked, methods of determining soil condition is a door-to-door "needs" survey. I know that many brave souls have had their knees turn to jelly at the mere mention of door-to-door survey. The "needs" survey is different. The singular objective of this survey is to discover the real and felt needs of your community. This is much less threatening to the participant than the survey that asks about church attendance or religious preference. In the "needs" survey, you will want to obtain certain basic information, such as the number of children at home and their ages. Beyond that, you want to discover needs.

For example, is there a need for a weekday child care? In an older community, a need might exist for an adult day-care center. You can use a simple one-question survey – "What need or needs exist in our community that you would like to see our church address?" You may have to give a few examples such as those above to prime the pump. You could also design a needs questionnaire based on the information you have already gathered and conclude it with the open-ended question mentioned above. People generally respond positively when they sense that someone is actually interested in listening to their ideas and meeting their needs.

Take the results of this information and begin to look at your program, facility, staff assignments, Bible study organization, and the like. Determine what you must do to meet the needs of the community. Be selective, no church can meet all of these needs. Move in the direction where you feel the strongest leading of the Lord. You will soon see results if you find a need and meet it.

The soil condition not only determines the kind of tree you can grow, but to some extent, the size of the tree. If the population of your community is 4,000, a mega-church model will only frustrate your people. You must establish ministry and growth goals that are realistic, given your soil conditions. Look for a role model among churches that are growing in soil conditions similar to your own. Learn from them. Study their programs and their organizational structure.

Once again, I would remind you that we should never use the soil conditions as an excuse for our lack of willingness to work at natural church growth. You can grow a church in any soil. You must first understand the soil and then plant the kind of church that will grow best in those conditions. The success of a church is not determined solely by its enrollment or attendance, but by its size and ministry relative to its given opportunity. True size is measured by the vision and heart to reach the local community and the world.

THE SUCCESS OF A CHURCH IS NOT DETERMINED SOLELY BY ITS ENROLLMENT OR ATTENDANCE, BUT BY ITS SIZE AND MINISTRY RELATIVE TO ITS GIVEN OPPORTUNITY. TRUE SIZE IS MEASURED BY THE VISION AND HEART TO REACH THE LOCAL COMMUNITY AND THE WORLD.

A Look at Your Own Soil

Occasionally, churches go through the process of looking at their community and then fail to look at the soil in their own pot. What is the makeup of the soil in your church? Some of the obvious questions are easy to answer, but frequently are overlooked.

Ask the Right Questions

What are the characteristics of your congregation in terms of age, race, gender, educational level, and so forth? These figures should then be compared with those discovered while studying your community. How do they correlate? What areas of opportunity have you overlooked? What must be done to reach those persons?

Let's look at an example. What if you discovered that your community had a growing population of young couples, but your church was composed primarily of older adults? With these facts in hand, you should see an opportunity to grow a young adult department. What then must you do? You must first develop classes for young adults or expand those you already have. You may need to allocate building space for preschool rooms. These rooms should be fresh, clean, and well-equipped. Young couples do bring preschoolers, and they are looking for a quality preschool program. Now develop a strategy for reaching the young couples. What do young couples enjoy doing? What events can we sponsor that will attract these young adults? I think you can see how to proceed.

In determining your own soil condition, you should go a step further by asking the simple question: "Who are we?" When I interviewed with the pastor search committee from First Baptist

Norfolk, I asked them that question.

One person responded: "We're not the rock church!"

I mused, *That's interesting, I wonder what material was used in building the church. Brick? Siding? Wood?* I soon discovered that he wasn't referring to building material. He was talking about a particular style of worship. The Rock Church was a large church in the community with a charismatic worship style. This man was trying to tell me that First Baptist was not charismatic in worship style or theology.

Another person responded: "We're not a typical First Church."

Once again I was curious. What is a typical First Church? For some that may imply liberal, rich, or exclusive. For others is may mean evangelistic, warm, or growing. It all depends on one's perspective and background.

I decided to rephrase my question. "If I was to visit your church and you were to visit me, what would you tell me about your church to encourage me to join?" Lights went on! One man responded that he would tell me that the church had a strong Bible-teaching program. Another added that he would tell me about the warm family atmosphere that pervaded the whole church body. Without realizing it, they told me something about their soil. It was fertile soil for Bible teaching and fellowship. I affirmed them in this and said, "Now we must tell the community who we are." It is more important to tell who we are than who we are not. What is your soil like? What do you do well? Does your community know that? How can you tell them?

Is Your Soil Soggy or Dry?

When examining your soil, I recommend another more penetrating step. You should look for soil conditions that stifle growth and those which could be hazardous to the life of the church. Dry soil comes from a lack of prayer and commitment and is manifested in a lack of joy, enthusiasm, and vision. Complacency sets in and people no longer expect the church to grow and reach the community for Christ. Worship and small group Bible study attendance are seen as duty and not privilege. People lose their excitement for inviting their friends to attend with them. The church withers in such dry soil.

A tree can survive dry soil longer than expected. One time, one of my prized bonsai trees was missed in the regular watering cycle for nearly a week. I had brought the tree indoors to decorate for a fellowship meeting and forgot it. When I discovered it, I was horrified. It had dropped its blossoms and the leaves had become brittle and dry. I was sure that is was dead. With my pruning tool, I trimmed one of the branches and found that it was still green and pliable below the bark. It was still alive! I put it outside and watered and fertilized it faithfully. In two weeks, the brittle leaves fell off and once again I thought all was lost. Yet I refused to give up and continued the watering and fertilizing. After several more weeks passed, I noticed that small light green leaf buds began to appear on a single branch. It was not long until the entire branch structure was covered with new leaves. The tree missed a flowering season, but it survived. Now it is healthy once again.

When a church allows its soil to dry out, it fails to bloom or produce fruit, but it can survive the drought. Perhaps the soil in your church has become dry. Growth has ceased and discouragement has set in. Your church need not die from the dry soil. Get on your knees together and ask God for a fresh anointing from His Spirit. Open God's Word and allow it to open you to His searchlight. Confess any and all sins He brings to your mind, turn from these, and make a renewed commitment to be the church. Dry soil can only be changed by the Father.

One other soil condition is hazardous to the health of the bonsai—soggy soil! Soggy soil will rot the root structure of the tree and soon the blossoms and leaves will fall. Soggy soil conditions are produced when the church becomes introverted, focusing on its own needs and desires, rather than fulfilling the Great Commission.

Root-rotting, soggy soil often occurs in the small group organization when a church fails to promote adults and to create new units for growth. Churches often excuse the failure to promote and create new units because of room constraints, convenience, the desire for intimate fellowship, and other assorted excuses. Whatever the excuse, stagnation in the small-group root structure of your church will ultimately dwarf it, or worse yet, choke off all life.

You can also cause root rot by too much emphasis on fellowship. A church should and must provide biblical fellowship and caring. We long for fellowship. Yet many churches allow coziness and cliquishness to masquerade for fellowship. Classes will often refuse to reach out to visitors, promote persons, or create new units because they don't want to dilute their fellowship.

True fellowship can never be diluted through numerical growth.

First John 1:1-4 teaches us that the conditions for meaningful fellowship are created by the sharing of the gospel. When a small group refuses to reach out to new persons because of the "wonderful fellowship" in their class, they are fooling themselves. They may have a close-knit clique, but they do not have meaningful fellowship. Conduct a simple test. Send a newcomer into the class for several weeks and then ask the guest to judge the warmth of the fellowship of that class. They'll often report that they felt excluded by the class. That's not fellowship! An overemphasis on "fellowship" will rot the roots.

An exaggerated emphasis on "quality" or "in-depth" Bible study can cause soggy soil. Often the request for an in-depth Bible study thinly covers an exaggerated and arrogant spirituality. "We're so spiritual and deep that we need a separate Bible study." Then we hear the common refrain-- "Those visitors just weren't serious about in-depth Bible study." Quality Bible study does not have to be obscure or exclusive. Jesus was a pretty deep teacher, but children, sinners, and other common persons found His teaching to be winsome. We must teach the Bible to win the lost and nurture the saints without excluding anyone. An exaggerated, proud emphasis on "in-depth" Bible study can choke out healthy growth.

Another condition that often creates soggy soil is the realization of the original dream. While you're scratching your head in confusion, let me illustrate. A mission church is planted with the dream that it will be self-supporting once they reach 100 in small group attendance, and establish a sound financial base. Soon the big day arrives and the mission constitutes and calls their first full-time pastor. The church breathes a sigh of relief because the original dream has been accomplished. Later, we look at that once rapidly growing mission and notice that it has stopped growing. They still have about 100 in attendance three years later. Why did the mission fail to continue its rapid growth curve? They failed to dream a new dream.

This factor can affect churches of all sizes. We had finished our fourth and apparently final building program at First Baptist Norfolk. (I say "apparently final" because we had saturated our existing property and no other land appeared readily available.) Yet we never know what God has in store. After the first three building programs, we always had an immediate and obvious growth spurt. In each of these programs, we built one phase of a master plan. In the last program, we completed construction of the entire master plan. We nearly doubled our floor space in that one project, but to our surprise, no spurt of growth followed. On the contrary, the church actually settled back slightly in small group attendance. Other pastors warned me concerning the post-building blues, but I didn't listen because it had never affected us before.

Why the lull this time? What was different? In this phase we completed everything we had on the drawing board. The dream had been realized. We had arrived! Now we could relax. Before we saw any renewed signs of growth, we had to dream a new dream. We had to renew the vision to reach people for Christ. We had to answer the question– "Where do we go from here?"

Changing Our Soil Condition

Its one thing to identify our soil condition, but quite another to change it. I've already indicated that dry soil can only be changed by God's Spirit as we get in the Word and in prayer.

If your church does not have an ongoing intercessory prayer ministry, begin one as quickly as possible. You can start with a few people who have a burden for the Great Commission and allow God to expand your prayer ministry in His own time. There are many helpful tools for establishing and growing an effective prayer ministry. You might want to look at the following resources and choose the one that would best serve your needs.

- *The Prayer of Jesus*, Ken Hemphill
- *Praying God's Word*, Beth Moore
- *Disciple's Prayer Life*, T.W. Hunt & Catherine Walker
- *Watchman Prayer Guide*, Larry Thompson
- *Prayer 101*, Elaine Helms

With the aid of the Holy Spirit, we can take several practical steps to change the soggy soil conditions which threaten to rot the root structure of our church.

Start by age-grading your entire small-group structure. If you have chosen to use another method of organization for small groups, ensure that new small groups are started and that there is a flow of new members into existing cells. Start a few new units. Nothing grows like new shoots. Help your people to understand the practical reasons for promotion and creating new units. Work together patiently and lovingly to accomplish these tasks. Change is always difficult and often painful.

Begin to reach out to unchurched and unsaved persons in your community. Nothing creates excitement in the church like new persons becoming involved. Put these new persons to work as soon as they are spiritually capable of serving. New people bring new ideas and they tend to break up the soggy condition of our soil.

You will need to work continually on attitudes and relationships within the church if you are to be successful in creating a good soil condition for healthy church growth. You need to face and correct negative attitudes such as those expressed in statements like— "Those newcomers are taking over our church," "Who do they think they are, we've worked hard for our church," and "The pastor just doesn't care about our needs, all he cares about is getting new members." These attitudes can be combated by creating an atmosphere where the impersonal relationships within the church are healthy. God's people need to learn to love one another.

Paul gave good advice for our relationships in Philippians 2:3-5: Do nothing from selfishness or empty conceit, but with humility of mind let each of you regard one another as more important than himself; do not merely look out for your own personal interests, but also for the interests of others. Have this attitude in yourselves which was in Christ Jesus.

Your church will grow if you ensure that the soil is healthy.

FERTILE THOUGHTS AND IDEAS

1. Take a close look at your community. Using the provided "Observation" sheet, as a starting point, what did you learn about soil?

2. In light of what you learned, what is your church doing right?

3. What changes need to be made in your soil conditions?

4. What are you willing to do personally to facilitate these changes?

5. Do you see signs of soggy or dry soil? What can be done to change these conditions?

5

CREATING AGE
AND DIRECTION

One of the most interesting techniques of the art of bonsai is that of creating the appearance of age and forcing the direction of growth. By stripping the bark from a particular limb, a tree can be made to look more ancient than it is. This illusion of age is intended to make the miniature tree look even more like its mature counterpart in nature. On a trip to Florida, I purchased a tree which had been made to look old. Upon returning, I proudly displayed it for my daughters. They liked the tree which appeared to be growing out of a rock, but they wanted me to cut off the dead limbs. "It makes it look like it's dying," they noted.

A second technique of mimicking the process of nature is to force the direction of growth by the use of wires. If you ever observe a collection of bonsai trees, you will no doubt notice that many of the limbs have been wrapped with copper wires. These wires force the tree to grow in a certain direction and configuration. A tree can be wired in such a way that it appears as if it has been windblown for years. It looks convincing, but it's all an illusion.

The Illusion of Fellowship

Many churches stay small because they have artificially created the illusion of fellowship. Small groups, which are not receptive to new persons and do not desire to create new units, often become introverted and their coziness bears a striking resemblance to authentic fellowship. But it is not the same! True biblical fellowship is created by the sharing of the gospel. Fellowship is ultimately a *by-product* of sharing the good news.

One of the greatest biblical passages on fellowship is found in 1 John 1. John wrote that we (believers) declare the things which we have seen, heard, and experienced that others may have fellowship with us and our fellowship is with the Father. Christian fellowship is both human and divine. Fellowship is *with God* and it is *with others*. True biblical fellowship must have both vertical and horizontal dimensions. John was concerned that unbelievers would experience Christian joy through fellowship with God. Further, he desired that the joy of believers would be enhanced as they share the gospel and new family members were added. We do not lose fellowship when we add new members to our group. True fellowship can never be diluted by numbers, only by complacency and sin.

Many churches remain artificially small under the guise that growth would dissipate fellowship. I think for some there is a genuine fear that natural growth will destroy the warmth they have come to treasure. For others, it is simply a selfish way of guarding their own personal interests. Many classes become cliques that have their own agenda and the newcomer is clearly made to feel unwelcome. These groups are usually reluctant to promote members to the correct age groups or to help start new units. They rarely encourage their own members to leave the class and serve elsewhere within the church family. They have only the illusion of fellowship!

We often associate fellowship with cook-outs, covered dish meals, social times or coffee and donuts before class. These events are important– adults need and desire to belong to a group. But biblical fellowship is much more than a list of class activities. Biblical fellowship demands interpersonal relationships where we can drop the mask we so often wear. A friend of ours recently told me of the lack of response by their class when they asked for prayer for their son's problem. Rather than responding to the need and embracing the couple, many in the class became aloof and virtually excluded them from fellowship. This class has an illusion of true fellowship!

Paul gave a graphic description of fellowship in 1 Corinthians 12:25-27:

> That there should be no division in the body, but that the members should have the same care for one another. And if one member suffers, all the members suffer with it; if one member is honored all the members rejoice with it. Now you are Christ's body, and individually members of it.

A speaker at Ridgecrest Conference Center near Asheville, North Carolina, once illustrated fellowship in action in a small group. This incident occurred in an adult Bible study class composed mainly of young professionals. The teacher committed the cardinal teaching "sin." He asked a relatively new member to read aloud the Scripture passage for that morning's lesson. The new member was a poor reader. He had difficulty reading the Bible aloud and stumbled on a number of words. The teacher thought he was having trouble pronouncing some of the words because he was reading from the *King James Version* and asked, "What translation are you reading?" The newcomer closed his Bible, looked at the cover, which had the word *concordance* written just below *Holy Bible*, and thoughtfully replied, "The Concordance Version." Not one of the highly education members laughed or even smiled. That was true fellowship.

The fellowship of First Baptist Norfolk was tested when men and women were called overseas because of the conflict in Desert Storm. The Sunday school classes and the entire church family responded with incredible speed. Letters and cards were written, support groups formed, and offers of assistance such as baby-sitting and household chores were abundant.

Fellowship does not occur simply because we have a room in our building dedicated to social dinners. Fellowship occurs only when the interpersonal relationships in the church are kept healthy.

Many classes have stripped the bark from the limb of their classes and they give an appearance of having fellowship, but they're not actually open to new members. Other classes are not interested in getting involved in the lives of fellow-members whether it leads to rejoicing together or suffering together. We're not after the appearance of fellowship, we're after the reality.

Sharing Authority

Christians often have an illusion of openness to new members only to slam the door when it appears that the newcomer decides to get involved. Existing members see the enthusiasm of new members as a threat to their own authority. Some people fear church growth because they enjoy being the big fish in a small pond. They really don't want to share their power. They give the illusion that they are overworked and want help, but when their authority is threatened they often strike out in such a way that the new member is made to feel unwanted.

We must all bear in mind that we have been called to service and not authority. All the credit and glory should go to Christ and not to any man. It would be incredible to think what we could accomplish together if no one was concerned about who had the authority and who received the credit.

Forcing the Direction

Many churches fail to grow to maturity because they artificially force the church in a particular direction. Bonsai enthusiasts wrap various size copper wires around the trunk and branches of a tree to bend them in a particular direction. This can give the impression that a tree has been blown over by the wind. The church has several different wires that are used to force direction.

The Wire of Tradition

The largest copper wire in our arsenal is that of tradition. When it's wrapped around the tree it says: "We've never done it that way," or perhaps "We've tried that before," or "It won't work here." We fear new ideas. We're afraid to try new things, to allow the Spirit to direct our growth. Since church growth is supernatural, we must be willing to allow the wind of the Spirit to move us as He wills. We cannot allow our traditions and our comfort zones to wire us into present patterns. Keep in mind that present traditions were once creative ideas of their own.

The Wire of Imitation

A second wire is altogether different. We can artificially force the direction of our church by modeling one church after another, without due consideration to the context of a particular situation. We can and must learn from other growing churches, but we cannot wire our church to be just like them. Like every individual is a unique creation of God; so each church is designed by the master architect. Don't believe it! Listen to this—"But now God has placed the members, each one of them, in the body, just as He desired" (1 Cor. 12:18).

I learned this the hard way while pastoring a small rural church in Wolf Creek, Kentucky. As soon as I arrived on the field, I started an aggressive evangelism training program. I had seen this program work well in my home church in Winston-Salem. I wanted to reach our community and this was the only model I knew. Thus, I forced my church in one direction for church growth – a direction for which they were not prepared and one which may not have been most suited to my new church field. To tell the truth, I had not spent sufficient time to discover the most suitable method for growing this church in the most efficient manner.

Every church must be willing to try new ideas with the understanding that not every idea will work. We must allow each other the freedom to "fail" if we are to ever succeed. Examine your community soil, learn from other churches, ask God to direct, and attempt something great for God. You never know what will work until you actually try something.

The Wire of Comfort

Another wire we use to force the direction of our church is the wire of comfort. "We like things the way they are. We're comfortable. We're making budget, paying the pastor; we get along quite well, thank you." This wire of comfort can cause the church to be restrictive in its thinking. "Those folks will never fit in here." "We like the convenience of a small church."

A prominent businessman in our community joined our church. Not long afterward he attended visitation and accompanied me on a visit. As the evening progressed, the couple being visited shared their testimony and began to ask questions about the church. I answered the inquiries and began to tell them about the wonderful programs we offered. The conversation flowed freely among the four of us. The businessman who was my visitation partner sealed the visit when he told why he joined the church.

He visited for several months before he decided to join. He liked the preaching, the choir and the programs, but he just wasn't sure he wanted to join and he didn't know why. One morning at the invitation, numerous people responded to join the church. Some were businessmen in nice suits, others were clean-cut young couples. Mixed in with the others was a young man with a pony-tail that stretched halfway down his back. He created quite a contrast. The businessman watched and to his surprise the church accepted everyone with equal warmth and joy. At that moment, he knew that he too must be part of a church that welcomed such a variety of persons. We refused to force the direction of our church with any artificial means.

We need not force the direction of our church's growth, we must move at the Spirit's direction to meet the needs of our community. The perfect bonsai creates an illusion. For all intents and purposes, it looks like its counterpart which has been left to grow naturally in its proper environment.

But your church is not intended to be an illusion. It is not a decorative miniature like the bonsai tree. It is the "real thing" created by God and placed in your community with the Great Commission in mind. Everything has been placed under the feet of Jesus for the sake of His church so that it might express God's fullness in the same way Jesus did during His incarnation (Eph. 1:18-23). It is sin when the church simply refuses to be all God designed it to be.

 FERTILE THOUGHTS AND ACTIONS

1. List situations which can create an illusion of fellowship.

2. What conveniences are keeping your small groups and church from growing?

3. Are there factors at work which are artificially forcing the direction of your church's growth?

6

THE DILEMMA OF THE BONSAI

The bonsai is a lovely piece of art, but it creates some unique dilemmas for the owner. Growing a bonsai in a ceramic pot can be a much more difficult task than growing a full-sized tree in its natural habitat. Did God call us to miniaturize His church, or to let Him grow it?

Cute, but Not Practical

As much as I love my collection of bonsai trees, I recognize that they do create several unique problems. First and most obvious, they are *ornamental*, but not *practical*. The little pot is lovely. The miniature tree looks like the real thing. In fact, I had a little tangerine tree that actually had tangerines. They were about the size of the tip of my thumb. They were not very edible or filling. That's the dilemma. The bonsai is cute, but it does not have a great deal of practical use to anyone. It's a piece of art. It can be used to decorate one's home, but that's about all.

When we artificially create a bonsai church, we get the same results. The building may have lovely stained-glass windows. The pot that holds the church may be a work of art, but the tree in that pot is not very functional when it comes to fulfilling the Great Commission.

God didn't call us to create a decorative piece of art; He called and empowered us to be a growing, living community. He called us to fulfill the Great Commission in our given area of responsibility. We cannot keep the church artificially small to satisfy our own personal desires or those of a few members. We must allow God to grow us to full maturity.

Believe it or not, it takes more effort to keep the bonsai small and alive than it does to grow a natural tree to its God-given potential. The same is true for the artificially small church.

Daily Watering

The size of the pot and the limitations of the root ball require that the bonsai be watered daily. When I was growing bonsai trees and went on a short journey, I had to get a baby-sitter for my bonsai trees. My wife jokingly commented that when I went away for a pastor's conference and called home, my first question was "Did you water the bonsai?" That's not true! I'm smart enough to ask Paula how she and the kids were before I asked about the trees. But, the fact is, my little trees required constant attention.

An artificially miniaturized church requires constant attention. The pastor is often called on to be a "hand-holder" rather than a Great Commission growth agent to reach the community. Sometimes the quip is heard: "Our pastor doesn't care for us, all he's interested in are those prospects." Translation: "We want him to water us daily." The miniature church is actually much more demanding than the naturally growing church. If I had taken the little pine tree I chose to bonsai and planted it in my yard, it would have taken much less daily care to grow in a natural, healthy manner. Further it would have served a practical function of providing shade.

The church that intentionally miniaturizes itself often develops a demanding attitude. Everything must be done to meet "my need." It becomes selfish and introverted. The church exists not only to meet the spiritual needs of its members, but also to reach the world for Christ.

Plucking off the Dead Needles

One of the most time-consuming tasks for the bonsai grower is the plucking of dead needles from pine trees. One of the tools in my bonsai arsenal is a pair of tweezers. To keep an evergreen bonsai healthy, the dead needles must be plucked from the tree. The miniature evergreen doesn't have the advantage of the forces of nature—wind, rain, and snow—which would naturally discard the needles if the tree were of normal size. On a regular schedule, I would spend countless hours seated at a table plucking tiny needles, one by one, from my tiny tree.

The miniaturized church demands constant needle-plucking. It rarely is exposed to forces of its own community. It is pampered and coddled with everything being done for it. Most of the money is spent on self-esteem items such as the pot or decorative items to showcase the pot. The members are called upon to do very little to ensure the healthy growth of their own church. They pay the pastor to do the work of ministry. The miniature church expects the pastor to pull away all the dead needles that could afflict them. He becomes the hired gardener of the church whose only function is to take care of "us."

The bonsai church will destroy the pastor's heart for evangelism and ultimately cripple his ministry. He will become frustrated with the tedious work of plucking away needles simply to keep everybody happy. Further, it will cause the church to lose its passion for soul-winning and become a miniaturized display model of the real thing. When we see the majesty of the church as the bride of Christ, we cannot allow it to be artificially miniaturized.

The Demand for a Greenhouse

No doubt you've already concluded that bonsai demand rather specialized care. This can be especially true during the winter. Since a bonsai is a real tree, it must experience the seasons which are natural to its annual development. I learned this the hard way when I kept a pine tree in my office throughout the entire year. It died, I was told, because it didn't experience the normal winter dormancy. Thus, a bonsai must have a winter rest, but it can't endure severe weather conditions. Its root depth is so shallow in the small container that it will easily freeze to death. This means that the bonsai demands a greenhouse for winter survival.

The church that has been kept artificially small frequently demands very specialized care. It is often controlled by one or two large family groups, and if the environment is not carefully controlled, major problems can occur and premature death can result. Churches are often "bonsaied" by families who have enjoyed exercising control by their money or influence in the community. They like the church the way it is! They're quite comfortable and well they should be – they run the church. When potential growth threatens their dominance, conditions can become quite hostile for the pastor or other newcomers.

God did not create the church for our pleasure or our control. It was not fashioned to make us comfortable. The church was created as the show place of God's manifold wisdom (Eph. 3:10). It was created to be His messianic community, extending the plan of redemption to the world (see Matt. 16:18). It is called to carry out the Great Commission (Matt. 28:19-20). Whose kingdom do we desire to build – our own or His?

A healthy, maturing church requires no greenhouse. It has been created by God with the resources to grow and withstand the onslaught of the adversary and the conditions of the environment. The gates of hell cannot stand against the church that is committed to be the church.

FERTILE THOUGHTS AND ACTIONS

1. Are there any symptoms that indicate that your church requires daily watering?

2. What are some ways to get people out of their comfort zones?

3. List the things your congregation will be willing to do, even if it is inconvenient, to reach people for Christ?

CHURCH GROWTH IS NATURAL AND SUPERNATURAL

The church is designed to grow. Jesus told His disciples: "I will build My church" (Matt. 16:18). The scriptural images of the church imply natural, healthy growth. The church is referred to as a field, a body, and a building in progress. Paul gave eloquent expression to this natural design for growth in 1 Corinthian 3:6-9.

> I planted, Apollos watered, but God *was causing the growth.* So then neither the one who plants nor the one who waters is anything, but God *who causes the growth.* Now he who plants and he who waters are one; but each will receive his own reward according to his own labor. For we are God's fellow workers; you are God's field, God's building.

In Ephesians 4:11-16, where Paul discussed the proper working of the gifted body, he concluded:

> But speaking the truth in love we are to *grow up in all aspects into Him*, who is the head, even Christ, from whom the whole body, being fitted and held together by that which every joint supplies, according to the proper working of each individual part, causes the growth of the body for the building up of itself in love (cc. 15-16).

The growth of the church is both natural and supernatural. The church was designed by God to grow *naturally*, but all church growth is a *supernatural* miracle. In truth, the church will experience growth if we remove artificial and selfish barriers we have used to keep our church artificially small – to keep it a bonsai church.

Defining the Bonsai Church

The conclusions of this study do not in any way imply that a small church is inferior to a large church. The bonsai church is a church which has been kept *artificially* small. Its natural growth has been hampered by human attempts to keep it small or inattention to the biblical pattern and methods for growth. Many methods can be used to keep a church small. Some of these bonsai techniques have been applied in ignorance of God's plan for church growth and others have been done from a selfish desire to be comfortable or control the church.

The bonsai church may be cute, but it's not practical. It is ornamental rather than fruit-bearing. It is a distortion of God's original plan.

Seeking God-given Size

The healthy church will grow naturally as God gives it growth. Further, a church's growth cannot always be measured by size alone. There are many species of trees. Some trees will grow to a larger natural size than will others. The redwood and the dogwood can hardly be compared.

We live in the era of the mega-church. Great attention has been given to very large churches. They certainly play a vital role in God's work in a given community. They must not be dismissed as inauthentic or mere expressions of the pastor's ego. If they are faithful to their commission, God Himself will provide for their growth. On the other hand, not every church should or could become a mega-church. A small community cannot support mega-church growth. The resources in terms of people are simply not available.

In 1972, I pastored a church in Wolf Creek, Kentucky, where the population was about 600. Our Sunday school grew to over 100 and we baptized 53 persons in 18 months. My next full-time pastorate was in Galax, Virginia. The church membership in Galax was actually larger than the entire population of Wolf Creek. In my third pastorate, the church membership was larger than the population of Galax. Neither Wolf Creek nor Galax could support a church of the size of First Baptist Norfolk. Therefore, church growth must be natural to the God-given size and opportunity.

CHURCH GROWTH MUST BE NATURAL TO THE GOD-GIVEN SIZE AND OPPORTUNITY

It is equally true that not all areas of the same community will yield equal growth opportunities. Some churches are located in transitional neighborhoods. They feel a strong call to continue to minister to that neighbor. The soil conditions in this transitional area may not be as conducive to growth as those in a growing suburban community.

There may also be different soil conditions in different areas of the country. Alabama, for example, may be more fertile than Wisconsin or Wyoming. Thus, church growth must be measured according to many environmental factors. It is nonetheless essential that every church seek to fulfill the Great Commission in the context of its God-given opportunity. We must be careful not to blame soil conditions for our own laziness or unwillingness to grow. I believe that the harvest in every area is more plentiful than we often believe. The issue for the non-growth of most churches is not the soil nor the seed but the lack of laborers (Matt. 9:37-38).

The church leadership must have a good understanding of the church's soil conditions and total environment. For example, a church in a community with many retirement-age persons needs to design programming aimed at reaching those persons. Frequently, I see churches develop a certain style of music program with little consideration to the particular tastes of their community. Since music is an essential component of the growing church, the worship team and church leaders must show sensitivity in developing a music and worship style which will reach and minister to people in their particular community.

Likewise, the small group organization must be developed with a view to the soil conditions. A church in a community densely populated with young adults should organize a large preschool department and think of events that would appeal to unsaved young adults.

Certain principles of church growth must be understood and utilized by every church[1]. There are many methods of applying these principles. Methodology may vary from situation to situation. The wise leader will utilize growth principles and discover those methods that work best in local soil conditions.

When A Tree Outgrows Its Pot

What do I do when a tree outgrows its pot? This is one of the most frequent questions I hear and rightly so since the pot is the most restricting element to natural growth. Some of the pots mentioned in this book can be easily replaced. If the church's vision is the restricting pot, pastor, ministry staff, and lay leaders can often find a greater vision by attending a growth conference or denominational training center. Another method is to visit a church with a similar soil condition that is showing healthy growth. We must learn from one another. Church growth is not a competitive sport, but a cooperative kingdom activity.

The pots of leadership and organization naturally go together. Ongoing leadership training is essential to the life of any healthy church. The expanding organization requires a sufficient number of well-trained leaders. The equipping of the laity for ministry appears to me to be the primary role of the pastor/staff (Eph. 4:11-12).

The most confining pot is that of land and building space. Short of new construction, space can be attained by multiple uses of the same facilities or the use of multiple sites. We may have to think outside the lines. The church is not restricted to Sunday morning at 11:00 for worship. Multiple use of the building is good stewardship because it provides virtually free space. Off-site space can often be found. The building of adequate space is a more normal solution to the space problem.

Land is a little more challenging. Dual hours for small groups, for example, will provide additional building space, but will in turn put even greater stress on available parking spaces. Parking structures have proved to be too costly for all but a few churches. Off-site parking is an option. A few churches have successfully used a park-and-ride system with a shuttle service. But it appears that most American church members are presently unwilling to make the sacrifice necessary to put up with this inconvenience. We are spoiled!

Some churches have solved the land problem by relocating. This is certainly *one* choice and may be the wisest choice in many situations. The church that relocates must ensure that the community being left will still be reached by an evangelical witness. Relocating is not the only solution. Many churches have decided that they will continue to grow through the planting of new churches in other areas of their community. Here, care should be taken to plant a healthy church that is committed to natural biblical growth (footnote 2). This church should be one that is suited to its new soil conditions. Church planting is a healthy method of church growth.

Growing In All Aspects

In Ephesians 4:15, Paul wrote that the church should grow *in all aspects* into Christ. Most church growth books point out the difference between biological, transfer and evangelistic growth. Biological growth comes from within. The church experiences this growth when it baptizes the children and youth of its own members. This is valid growth and every church should seek to reach its own. Transfer growth occurs when individuals transfer their membership from another church, either from outside the present community or within. This too is valid church growth, but must not be allowed to degenerate into "sheep stealing." These two forms of numerical growth should not be the only form of church growth.

Every church must be involved in evangelistic growth. Somewhere, the idea has crept in that some churches are not called to have an evangelistic ministry. We must recognize that there is a natural variety among churches even as there is variety in the trees of nature. Yet the church, by definition, must be evangelistic. The church cannot fulfill the Great Commission without an evangelistic outreach to its community. Evangelistic growth is natural to every church. Each church must be intentional and persistent in its commitment to reach the lost.

EVANGELISTIC GROWTH IS NATURAL TO EVERY CHURCH.

Beyond these three forms of numerical growth, there are other forms of growth. There must be growth in biblical knowledge and moral standards. Churches must grow through the development of Christian character in their membership. There are growth issues which relate to greater mission awareness and stewardship. This will often lead to mission involvement both in and beyond one's community. Many churches who have reached the saturation point in their existing setting have found new life by looking beyond their community and developing a heart for the reaching of the nations. They invest in ministry projects in their community and take their people on mission trips beyond the borders of their state. They are often surprised and delighted to find that this "outward" focus gives new life to the local church.

As you can see, not all church growth is numerical growth. Yet, I must again add a word of caution. Numerical growth should not be discounted or ignored. Churches often avoid the matter of numerical growth by arguing that they emphasize other forms of growth.

Church growth is not either/or but both/and. Avoiding the topic of numerical growth is often a defense mechanism for laziness, lack of commitment, or desire to remain comfortably small. It is one of the leading causes of bonsai churches.

God desires to build your church. This doesn't necessarily mean it will become a mega-church. It does mean that your church must grow to take full advantage of its God-given opportunities. Arthur Flake, a layman who wrote about Sunday school growth nearly a century ago, wrote:

> **There is inspiration in numbers, but let it be understood that a school does not necessarily have to have an enrollment of 1,000 members to be a great school. It may be a really great school and have an attendance of a hundred or even less. However, no Sunday school is worthy of being called a great school unless it is reaching a large majority of the people who should attend it. This is true no matter what other claims to efficiency it may have.** [3]

What Flake said in 1922 is equally true today. Your church is responsible for reaching a large majority of those who should attend. As long as there are lost

YOUR CHURCH CAN GROW!

and unchurched people in your community, your church has work to do. Your church can grow!

⊘ FERTILE THOUGHTS AND ACTIONS

1. Briefly describe your understanding of the biblical model of church growth using the Scriptures mentioned in this chapter.

2. What soil conditions are affecting your church's ability to grow?

3. What are the factors in your worship services that are affecting your ability to grow?

4. Is there a particular age group in your community that your church should be providing ministries for which it currently is not providing?

5. List the available opportunities to provide additional space and land around your church's facilities. Should your church consider relocating in order to fulfill God's challenge for your church's ministry?

6. How evangelistic is your church? What can be done to improve the evangelistic climate of your small groups and church? List some practical steps that you are willing to do to see that this is accomplished.

Footnote 1: Ken Hemphill, *The Antioch Effect: 8 Characteristics of Highly Effective Churches* (Nashville: Broadman & Holman, 1994).

Footnote 2: Jack Redford, *Planting New Churches* (Nashville: Broadman & Holman, 1978).

Footnote 3: Arthur Flake, *Building a Standard Sunday School* (Nashville: The Sunday School Board, 1922), 28.

8

GROWING A
NATURAL TREE

What do I do now? How do I get started growing a healthy, natural tree? Perhaps these questions have entered your mind as you have read this book.

Congratulations

Congratulations! You have already made a valuable beginning. Participating in the study of this book indicates your interest in healthy church growth and your willingness to learn how to grow your church. You have already started dealing with the pot of limited vision. Now you need to help communicate this vision to others in your church.

If you are a layperson, you will want to begin with your pastor. Share this book with him or give him a copy that he can read and mark. Ask him if you can discuss these concepts with him after he has completed the book. Pray for him while he is reading the book. The pastor is called by God to lead the church; therefore, it is essential that he share the vision for church growth. It has been my experience that a majority of pastors want to see their church grow. He will be delighted to have your encouragement. If he is somewhat reluctant to move ahead, be patient and allow God to bring conviction to this area.

If you are a pastor, you will need to communicate these ideas to your congregation. God has called you to provide the leadership for your congregation. This will give you an excellent opportunity to provide that visionary leadership. I have found that most lay persons want to see their church grow once they understand the principles of biblical church growth.

People often fear that which they do not understand. The more that you can do in the way of communication, the better will be the results. Free small group Bible study guides are available online at auxanopress.com. As you participate in the book study, encourage open discussion and saturate the group time with prayer. I would encourage you to begin this process with those who have been elected to leadership positions by the church. If these trusted laypersons adopt these growth ideas, they can help you communicate them effectively to the rest of the congregation.

Above all, be patient and prayerful. These ideas may meet with some resistance in the beginning simply because they are new. Ask God to create receptivity.

Keep Growing

This book, by design, only introduces the topic of church growth. The more you can read, the better prepared you will be to lead your church to grow. You will find any number of books on church growth at your local Christian bookstore. If you encounter resistance when discussing the idea of church growth, you might begin with the 40 day study entitled *Eternal Impact: The Passion of Kingdom Centered Communities*. It focuses on the book of Acts and several passages from the Pauline letters which describe God's design for His church.

Attend a Church Growth Conference

Church growth and small group conferences are held in nearly every area of our country. You can find one near you. Begin with denominational resources. They are usually less expensive than those sponsored by various churches or growth organizations. Often they will be tailored to the specific needs of your church. Do not, however, avoid other conferences simply because of the cost. They are a good investment in your ministry and your church's work. Participating in a growth conference allows you to interact with others who have experienced problems similar to those you are facing. The conference also provides a contagious spirit of excitement that you cannot catch from reading a book.

Talk to Those Who Have Done It

Church growth is not a competitive sport, but a cooperative ministry. When you discover another church that is doing a good job at reaching its community for Christ, set up an appointment to talk to the pastor or staff. I can tell you from experience that they will be delighted to share any lessons they have learned. I have gained greatly from talking to those who have done it. Those who are committed to church growth principles in their own church want to see your church grow, too. Don't hesitate to ask for help.

Make a Commitment to Biblical Growth

Church growth is natural, but not easy. It is a lifelong process that requires continual planning, implementation, and plain hard work. It is worth it because church growth enables the church to fulfill the Great Commission. If you're going to stay with growth principles during the difficult times, you must make a commitment to be a church-growth agent. The biblical images concerning the church imply growth. The Great Commission mandates that the church reach those who are unsaved. This will provide natural, healthy church growth. Don't be discouraged if your church doesn't explode overnight. Be patient! Growth principles work, but they may take time. The soil where the church is planted may not yet be receptive to the gospel. Use your Sunday school or small group structure to focus on evangelism. Remember, prayer is the key to changing the receptivity of the soil.

Growth is a supernatural activity of God in which He graciously allows us to participate. You can be the instrument through whom God works to accomplish His activity on earth. Paul referred to himself as a servant through whom the Corinthians believed as God gave him the opportunity (1 Cor. 3:5). What opportunity has God placed before you and your church?

Look at Your Pots

If, through reading this book, you have discovered some "small pots" that are constricting the growth of your church, begin to take the steps to resolve your problem. If you need building space immediately, consider multiple sites or times for worship and small groups. The use of multiple Sunday schools will provide additional time to begin the building planning process.

You must enlarge the small group organization and leadership first, if you intend for your church to grow. I recommend age-grading your small group structure. This will enable guests to your small groups to readily identify their class. Age-grading also provides the most natural method of enlarging the small group organization. For example, you may begin with a small group for persons from 20 to 29 years of age. When the enrollment of this class exceeds 30 you could start a new teaching unit by dividing the class into two classes. One could be for those 20 to 24 and the other for those 25 to 29. This will help you to expand your organization and maintain the integrity of your grading system. The age-grading system also recognizes the common needs that are shared by those of similar age and life stage.

If you choose another system for organizing your small groups, make sure the system allows for natural growth through the creation of new units and the natural movement of persons. It should be a system that allows for systematic and natural reorganization to accommodate growth. It should be simple enough to communicate to a first time attendee.

You cannot enlarge the organization without enlarging your pool of leadership. Leadership enlistment and training is an ongoing task of the growing church. Use variety and creativity in the solicitation of leaders. The best method of leadership recruitment is one-on-one. Most listeners think that the announcements from the pulpit are intended for someone other than themselves. Leaders must be prayerfully approached on an individual basis. Ask God to lead you to the right persons for leadership training. Pray that God will prepare their hearts before you approach them. Ask them to pray about the opportunity for service in a particular area. Assure them that the church will provide adequate training. Set a date to get together to discuss their decision for service.

A good source for discovering potential leaders is those presently serving as leaders. Encourage your teachers to help you recruit other leaders. This process will not work unless your existing leaders are committed to church growth through the small groups. If small group leaders see their class as their personal property, they will be reluctant to encourage class members to serve in other positions. It is important that leaders of the church have a Great Commission consciousness. I think it would be a good plan to ask your teachers to attempt to recruit another person to work as their "associate" with a view to full-time service. Ask each small group leader to recruit one additional person who could teach in their age division. They could then invite them to sit in on the class for a few weeks as an observer.

You must provide adequate training to experience healthy growth. Today's fast-paced environment requires that the church use a variety of methods for teacher training. You can offer training for one night a week for eight or ten consecutive weeks. This works well for some people's schedules. You might also try a Friday night/Saturday morning training blitz. We have discovered that many persons are more likely to give up one evening and one morning than they are to commit to extended training periods. Some churches hold "midnight madness" training events. They begin at seven o'clock and continue until midnight. You should give participants a break during the evening and provide refreshments. Try it, you might like it! You will be amazed at how much training can be done in one evening.

You must be willing to do whatever is necessary to secure and train adequate leadership because this is the key to natural church growth. After the initial training, you should provide regular training and encouragement. Many churches find it helpful for small group leaders to meet on a weekly basis to discuss the Bible study material and pray for the needs of class members. Whatever the cost, the results will be well worth the sacrifice.

Nurture the Root Structure and Encourage New Growth

Simply refuse to prune the root structure of your church. When you discover inactive persons on your church or small group rolls, don't remove them; go get them. I have discovered that many of those people who are chronically inactive in church may never have accepted Christ as their personal Savior. They may have joined the church or a small group without fully understanding the good news of the gospel. Don't lose your opportunity to share the gospel with these persons by tossing their name in the trash can. Others may have become inactive out of apathy or through hurt feelings. In either case, these persons must be lovingly cared for by their Christian family.

Develop programs for encouraging new members. Every church, regardless of size, needs a new-member orientation class. This class can be taught by the pastor, ministry staff or a layperson under his supervision. This class can be a simple one-session orientation to the church, or it can be a more structured and more intensive class designed to cover such matters as church history, distinctive doctrines, membership responsibilities, ministries offered, and other such matters as deemed necessary to responsible church membership. Try to involve every new member in a small-group Bible study. Members who do not get attached to a small-group through the church have less connection to the church. They are easily "pinched off."

While pastoring, I invited all the new members to my home once a month for an informal fellowship time. This allowed to them meet me and my family and ask questions about the church. This is another way to ensure that the new growth is not pinched from the tree. Find a place of ministry involvement for new members as quickly as possible. Many churches miss golden opportunities to utilize the spiritual gifts of new members by failing to involve them in the ministries of the church quickly. New members often demonstrate greater enthusiasm for their newfound church home than do those who have been part of the church for a longer period of time. Capitalize on this natural and healthy excitement.

Ensure that all of your small groups schedule regular fellowship events. These need not be elaborate. A simple covered-dish dinner will suffice. Allow ample time for conversation and ensure that no one is excluded. These class fellowships provide informal time for building relationships that is often lacking on Sunday morning due to the time constraints.

Focus on Evangelism

One factor that growing churches have in common is a clear focus on evangelism. The Great Commission establishes evangelism as the first priority of the church. The church that understands its primary mission in terms of this scriptural mandate will be a healthy, growing church. Focusing on evangelism will not compromise the quality of your pastoral care ministry or water down your fellowship. On the contrary, the focus on soul-winning enhances the other ministries of the church. Evangelism is the engine that drives biblical church growth.

There are many tools that can help you develop an intentional evangelistic strategy. The key is that each church must be intentional and find a strategy that God uses in their context. Start by encouraging your people to pray for lost persons by name. Encourage everyone to bring lost people with them to their small group or to a church function. Year after year we discover that a great majority of people who become involved in a particular church do so because they were brought by a friend or relative.

Your Church Can Grow

God has provided all the resources necessary for balanced church growth. Your church can be an exciting part of God's plan for world redemption. Allow God to remove the restraints which have kept your church from growing naturally in a supernatural way.

ABOUT THE AUTHOR

KEN HEMPHILL

Ken Hemphill has pastored churches throughout the Southeast, served ad a denominational leader within the Southern Baptist Convention for over twenty years, has been recognized as a leader in church growth and health, and presently serves as National Strategist for Empowering Kingdom Growth. Later this year, Ken will become the founding director of the Center for Church Planting and Revitalization at North Greenville University.

KENNETH PRIEST

Kenneth Priest serves the Southern Baptists of Texas Convention on the Church Ministries Team working with churches in revitalization and church health. A second-chair leader and background as a minister of education, Kenneth has served churches in Texas and North Carolina.